SURVIVING
YOUR BOSS

SURVIVING YOUR BOSS

HOW TO COPE WITH OFFICE POLITICS AND GET ON WITH YOUR JOB

Ann D. Clark, Ph.D.
and Patt Perkins

A CITADEL PRESS BOOK
Published by Carol Publishing Group

A Citadel Press Book
Published by Carol Publishing Group
Citadel Press is a registered trademark of Carol Communications, Inc.
Editorial Offices: 600 Madison Avenue, New York, N.Y. 10022
Sales and Distribution Offices: 120 Enterprise Avenue, Secaucus,
    N.J. 07094
In Canada: Canadian Manda Group, One Atlantic Avenue, Suite 105,
    Toronto, Ontario M6K 3E7
Queries regarding rights and permissions should be addressed to
Carol Publishing Group, 600 Madison Avenue, New York, N.Y. 10022

Carol Publishing Group books are available at special discounts for
bulk purchases, sales promotion, fund-raising, or educational
purposes. Special editions can be created to specifications. For
details, contact: Special Sales Department, Carol Publishing
Group, 120 Enterprise Avenue, Secaucus, N.J. 07094

Manufactured in the United States of America
10   9   8   7   6   5   4   3   2   1

Library of Congress Cataloging-in-Publication Data

Clark, Ann D.
    Surviving your boss : how to cope with office politics and get on
with your job / Ann D. Clark and Patt Perkins.
        p.   cm.
    ISBN 1-0-8065-1803-0 (pbk.)
    1. Office politics. 2. Interpersonal relations. 3. Conflict
management. 4. Managing your boss.   I. Perkins, Patt, 1932–
II. Title.
HF5386.5.C57   1996
650.1′3—dc20   95–47096
                                                          CIP

To our families: our children, the employees of today; our grandchildren, the hope for the future and the employees of tomorrow.

Contents

Preface

This book is about how to survive in the workplace without being eaten alive. It is a simple, practical, and workable approach to breaking out of the terror that so many employees face each day. Terror can take the form of a tyrannical boss, an alcoholic supervisor, job insecurity, unreasonable demands for time and effort. This adds to the stress already created by juggling home and family, the loss of "a life," and personal sacrifices that have become deadly. We tell you how to take control of your job and end the malaise that affects your daily productivity, both in and out of the workplace.

Surviving Your Boss is about real people with explosive problems who are trapped in what feels like a combat zone. It is about how to create choices when none seems to exist. It is about ways to come to terms with the hostility that employees direct toward their bosses or turn inward, causing ill health and unhappy home lives. It is about amnesty, creating a demilitarized zone, and acceptance—with specific exercises and techniques designed to reduce animosity and anger, and thus the possibility of a violent response.

The authors of this book are also employees. We've been there when that last straw was descending . . . the back breaker. We will talk to you in understandable terms, giving real accounts of workers revealing their frustrations. The stories will support readers by relating to their own dilemmas—you are not alone! And frustration and futility are not the end of the experience. This book will give you practical, efficient methods of regaining personal power in the workplace.

The loss of personal control in the workplace is exactly what invokes the worker to strike out through crime—from petty pil-

fering to sabotage of expensive computer systems—and even violence, tragically leading to death. In bottom-line terms, resentment in its various forms costs American employers over $800
million a week. The cost is borne by the worker, not just the
stockholders. This book is for bosses too. It tells you how to stop
the cycle of anger—for every boss *is* a worker and every boss has
a boss!

Surviving Your Boss will discuss methods for coping with difficult behavior (some, your own) and how to put into practice
workplace survival techniques.

In chapters 1 and 2 the parameters of economic, corporate,
and contemporary job stress are defined. Case studies and anec-
dotes will help you, the reader, to identify with others whose difficulties parallel your own.

Chapter 3 looks at the boss as an employee with a boss. Six
types of difficult bosses are identified, with strategies for working
with each and coping with their frustrating and intimidating characteristics.

Chapters 4, 5, 6, and 7 identify the workplace dynamics that
predominate where individuals feel uneasy, distressed, and
oppressed on the job. The relationships between workstyle personality, addictive systems, codependency, and anger, with its
underlying base of fear, are addressed, and action steps, coping
behaviors, and an emphasis on increased understanding of self as
a component in each of these dynamics are discussed.

Chapters 8, 9, and 10 address issues of anger, health, stress,
safety, and ethics. Again, specific and practical responses are
described.

Chapter 11 summarizes your commitment and tells you how
to stay motivated, how to assure follow-through, and how to maximize your probability of success.

At the end of each chapter is an action section labeled "the
Three Rs." Just as the basics of reading, writing, and arithmetic
form the basis of education, the Three Rs, "recognize, respond,
and reinforce," form the basis of your plan for change, comfort,
and control—in order to get on with the job!

Acknowledgments

Although this book contains over 60,000 words, there are never enough to thank the many who have freely given time, support, and encouragement. First, to Tandice Tinney, whose diligence in word processing, faxing, editing, and patiently transcribing hours of tape, made this book real, sincere thanks. To Deanna Lynne Smith, whose creativity and criticism helped hone the final form, heartfelt appreciation. To Terri Price and Colin Klett for their valuable technical advice and personal support, our gratitude. To the many interviewees, bosses, and employees alike, thank you for the generous gift of your stories, time, and insights. To the corporations that have contributed to the ideas in the book, to the great employees who work there, and to the families who support them, thank you all.

Your success depends on you
You have to steer your own course
You have to do your own thinking
You must make your own decisions
You have to solve your own problems
Your character is your own handiwork
You have to write your own record
You have to build your own monument—
   or dig your own pit.
Which are you doing?

B. C. FORBES

SURVIVING YOUR BOSS

ONE

Out of Control

"Self-generated discipline now challenges the power of bureaucratic structure, ushering in an era of individual freedom. There is now hope that the individual can rise above bureaucracy and preside over it."

FREDERICK G. HARMON

THE DYSFUNCTIONAL WORKPLACE

How often do you, as an employee, cope with disruptive forces in the workplace? Mergers, layoffs, unscheduled overtime, inconveniences, and changes that must be dealt with on a minute-by-minute basis are only a few of the challenges you face at work. It makes little difference whether you've worked on a project or a job for a few hours or a number of years. The boss walks by and gives the order that upsets the status quo. The company closes its doors with no notice. Uncertainty creates a sense that there is no control. Surely you have none!

Do you wonder if hard work and dedication pay off? Are these concepts that have gone out of fashion like a '70s Nehru jacket? "Sure, I like my job," you respond without hesitation, *"but what about the boss?"* Uncaring? Unconcerned? Unbearable? How can you quit? You're not working here for your health. Besides,

1

you're doing a good job. Even though you've never been late and you're faster than the others who perform the same tasks, you've never once gotten a compliment. Often you feel like you're treated as part of the equipment. You have no control.

Sometimes we protest. Sometimes we take out the frustration and anger in subtle ways. Have you left a customer waiting, a telephone ringing, taken long lunches, swiped pencils, not because you needed to, but somehow it soothed your anxiety? You fought back. You felt some sense of justice. You felt, if only for the moment, *in control.* And what about the other workers and your work environment? Do you feel like there's a gloomy cloud hanging among the employees? Are you personally affected by the negative games played within your company and by your boss? Real workers, just like you, talk about their powerlessness. Listen for a moment to this "tale of two companies." You are not alone.

A TALE OF TWO COMPANIES

"I have the perfect job," says Theresa, a petite brunette in trendy clothes. "Well . . . *had* it. I was a receptionist for a large defense contractor." Married to a state trooper, Theresa had a job that complemented his schedule and gave her time to be with their son, a senior in high school. "I worked four and a half days per week and was paid a significantly higher wage than the average receptionist. I had good equipment, friendly coworkers, minimum supervision, and excellent benefits. It really was a perfect job. Not only did I think it was perfect, I thought it was permanent. I had held the job for over five years. Because I didn't want to go back to school, I was willing to be a career receptionist. I didn't want to upgrade. I didn't want a promotion. In some ways I thought this assured me of keeping the job. No one could be jealous of me and no one could want my job. What a surprise when the company announced a major reorganization!"

With no notice, Theresa was given two choices. She would now work five days a week and have more work. No more half days off. Her hourly salary was to be cut, and with the increased workload she got more supervision. Her job skills were no longer adequate for the new supervisor. She received frequent oral and written warnings. Her life became a nightmare. How did this happen? Overnight she went from being the perfect employee with the perfect job to the employee from hell with the job from hell! Theresa now faces a tight job market with limited skills and the possibility of a poor reference. Or, she can endure.

Vic tells a different story, but he and Theresa have much in common. "To me being called a workaholic was a compliment," he said. "I worked sixty to eighty hours a week as a vice president for a large corporation providing software to the automotive industry. Vice president was a level of promotion that I never thought I would achieve because I had no college or formal training. I was a good salesman and I knew the product. As the marketplace began to change, there was more competition and foreign intrusion. Our company fell into what I can only describe as a panic, and that panic resulted in severe demotions everywhere."

Vic continued, "Company cars were taken away. Expense accounts were monitored. I was demoted, not just to a level below vice president, but down to a middle manager. Overnight I lost my company car, my laptop, my travel privileges, my secretary—all the perks of my job. And with it, my self-esteem! I became just another employee, and all the years of faithful service, the sixty-to-eighty-hour weeks, the total disruption of my family life, the dedication that I had to this job and this company were rewarded by the most incredible punishment."

Like Theresa, Vic experienced shock in the form of an abrupt realization that any security he had in his job was an illusion. Both Vic and Theresa had attempted to secure their places in the corporation, both worked hard and competently. Theresa believed her modest expectations assured her continued employment. Vic believed his "more is better" philosophy of workaholism gave him job security. Both felt untouchable and secure—in control.

AT WAR

These two stories dramatically exemplify how the workplace can often become a battlefield for the employee. It follows too often that the employee then becomes the enemy in the workplace. These two employees felt that they had significant control over their jobs. They both felt that hard work, job competency, that loyalty would result in certain guarantees. They felt like they had a "deal." They quickly learned that the other party had not signed on the dotted line of that deal. The workplace that Vic and Theresa have just described was a haven for them, providing not only the money that supported their lifestyle and enhanced their family, but also choices and options. Yet, overnight, the jobs became nightmarish—the employees felt trapped and powerless. Overnight, they came to hate the jobs that they had previously loved.

All too often an employee sees the workplace as a battleground and himself or herself as a soldier in the trenches, unable to control his or her own life because of very disruptive forces: economics, business trends, competition, foreign intrusion, or simply poor decision-making and mismanagement. It is the uncertainty and powerlessness that drives workers out of control.

The Crime Prevention Manual for Business Owners and Managers warns that any given business may be losing as much as a third of its profits to internal crime and employee sabotage. Additionally, as many as 30 percent of all business failures are a direct result of *internal* theft, often due to employee discontent. So, why doesn't management listen? Why are stories like those of Vic and Theresa so common? And what about the other workers and their morale? Do you feel like there's a gloomy cloud hanging among the employees in your company? Are you personally affected by negative games played against the company and your boss? Do you hate "politics"? Let's look further.

TAKING CONTROL

With the information contained in this book you can understand the dynamics of the workplace so you can feel more appreciated and less like a pawn. You will find practical suggestions and exercises to help you discover personal power. You will learn ways to excuse your boss (or the company, or the CEO) so you can do your best. And you will be healthier and happier if you give up anger at your boss and get on with the job.

Taking control may be a simple process: step-by-step assessment, planning, and choices. But it is not easy. Following the steps in this book, you will learn:

- You are not alone.
- You *can* redesign your job.
- You can take control of your emotions.
- The action steps of empowerment.
- Your own success depends on you.
- You can build your own monument.

THE SUGGESTION BOX

Janice tells the story of corporate directives to save money. When Janice received the corporate edict stating that thousands of dollars had to be cut from the upcoming budget, she took very seriously her responsibility to come up with ideas for saving money. She met with her team and several good suggestions came forward. One of these suggestions included placing restricted phone lines in conference rooms where Janice had observed workers frequently making personal phone calls. With about twenty conference rooms, or twenty "free phones," in her building, she felt this could make a significant difference. Janice even went to the trouble of tallying the workers who entered a conference room area near her in order to document the possibility of savings.

Janice provided both her data as well as a suggestion for a review of the phone records for these conference rooms. Based on simply attributing a local toll call to the total number of unauthorized entrances to the conference rooms she came up with a significant $2,500 saving for just one conference room. Janice was very proud of her analysis and initiative. She and others had submitted their reports for budgetary control to their own bosses.

Several months later there was still very little feedback. But the increasing stinginess of the company became apparent. Janice was not allowed to replenish supplies, people were told to use pencils when they ran out of pens. There was a level of pettiness that seemed to agitate the workers and interfere with job performance.

Janice then went to her supervisor to ask about the status of her suggestion for controlling telephone use in the conference rooms. He informed her he had passed it on. She asked him to follow up. He said he would. Weeks again went by. Morale was increasingly low. Janice decided to approach the chief financial officer of the company in a casual and joking way to ask about her suggestion. The CFO was a very approachable man; unusual, Janice felt, for a "business type." She had luckily encountered him in the hallway where she could casually ask if he had taken a look at her proposal.

The CFO laughed. "What if some bigwig wants to make a call, Janice?" he said. "What are we supposed to do? Tell him that we are saving money and they can't use our long distance lines?" Janet smiled and felt her cheeks turn red. She believed that her suggestion may have been laughed at behind closed doors. Janice made some light response and retreated.

She went back to her office cubicle and felt like crying. She wondered how she could have been so misunderstood. As she sat feeling humiliated and somewhat ashamed, she began to experience another feeling: anger. She pictured an upper level of management, cigar-smoking, scotch-drinking, immaculately groomed executives standing in the conference rooms, contemptuous of employees, contemptuous of money, contemptuous of the small savings that Janice and her coworkers had envisioned as being helpful to the overall mission of the company.

Her anger and her rage grew. She sat in her office for a long time. She plotted various forms of revenge. She saw herself going into the conference room and placing long distance calls to friends across the country. She saw herself dialing random numbers so the calls couldn't be traced back to her. She sat for yet a longer time plotting, something that would make her feel more equal to these contemptuous men in their expensive suits. In an exchange that had taken only minutes, Janice had changed from a dedicated, goal-directed employee to an angry, resentful, and hostile team dropout.

Have you ever felt like Janice? As a worker, how often do you think that instability of the workplace makes it feel more like a battleground than a place to perform your duties? You try to rationalize their ideas. You try to talk it out with your supervisor. "Gee, boss, we sure would like some time on this one . . . could we talk about how this will affect our work on the project . . . do you have a few minutes," you ask in your most confident, responsible voice. For moments that stretch to what feels like hours, you begin to feel droplets of sweat form on your brow, and you wait for the affirmative answer: "Sure, come in to the office right now. I've been wondering what you think."

Then your eyes meet. There's the "who-the-hell-do-you-think-you-are" look in the boss's eyes. You instinctively know that means the decision has come down from the top. "I can't do anything about it," comes the remark as your boss fiddles and restacks the papers on the desk. There's no possibility for an alteration in the program. The order is given. So you walk back to your work area, frustrated and disenchanted.

A part of the scenario you might have missed is seeing the helpless emotion that crossed your boss's face when you left the room. She sat there muttering, "Gee, I know how it feels, but I've got my orders too. I'm stuck in the middle, just like the employee. I'm higher up? Sure, but without other coworkers to share the responsibility and resentments. Nobody ever sympathizes with me!"

It's not realistic to generalize. Hey, it happens to everybody. That's life! Some workers handle such conflicts with aplomb. However, the truth is that those feelings of anger, frustration, and powerlessness are shared by a large portion of the workforce. You're not alone if you've lashed out at an employer's total disregard for you. Or if you've stuffed those feelings of resentment, increasing personal stress, and discomfort. How often do you feel the pressure and workload of the job seize control of your mind? Do you force your mind and body to behave in ways that go against your personal value system? How frequently have you experienced the terror of not knowing if you'll be let go, publicly ridiculed, or intimidated by your boss? Are you sick and tired of feeling like a soldier lost in the trenches while World War III blazes above?

A No-Win Situation

Connie is a single mother with two kids at home and she'll be ready to retire in five years. About three months ago, she heard through the grapevine that the plant would be opening a new facility inland . . . about one hundred miles away. "I worked twenty years for this really big snack food manufacturer. Toiled my way from the absolute lowest rung on the ladder into management. I'm proud of my accomplishment. It's taken dedication and pride in my work."

As she spoke, Connie bit her lip and focused on the scene in her driveway, her daughters soaping up the family's elderly station wagon. "When I heard the rumor from a reputable source, I talked it all over with the kids, and we agreed that changing high schools wouldn't be great, especially for Heather, who is a senior. But we're a family. We'd handle it. But when my boss finally called me into her office, I was told I wasn't going to be one of the people to move. They were demolishing my job. After twenty devoted years, I was 'phased out.' "

Connie stopped and twisted a button on her sweater. "They wouldn't need me in the new facility even though I wanted to go. I was willing to sell our family home, transplant my kids, change churches, and be unable to see my elderly parents as often. I was willing to sacrifice all that, and they still didn't care." Connie hesitated for a moment, squaring her shoulders. She was obviously a women who had mastered plenty of hurdles. "The boss said she understood and gave me a choice knowing that

I'd lose my retirement and health benefits if I quit. They also offered me a year's severance pay . . . but no health benefits. They [the bosses higher up] started to hassle me. I'm too expensive to have on the payroll, I guess. But I continued to concentrate on my job.

"Then they made me this 'generous offer.' I could stay with the plant in San Francisco, but go back to the graveyard shift working in quality control . . . on a twelve-hour shift, no less. Since I was still management, it was somehow okay for me to work twelve hours straight. Sure I'm angry. But I'm going to stick it out. What real alternative do I have?" She went on, "I know it's not my boss's fault. She's just taking her orders from the management, who get their orders from the CEO, who then has to answer to the accountants or stockholders, who only see the bottom line. Sure, it's not fair, but that's business. Anyhow, who ever said that a company should be fair?"

Connie stopped talking. She rubbed her lips with the back of her fist, took a breath, and continued. "About a week after going back on the night shift, manufacturing potato chips, I started to reject every other batch of chips as they passed by me on the conveyor belt. I've been with the company so long, if I said they weren't right, not up to our quality standards, nobody even thought to question my decision. There was nothing wrong with them. The chips were fine, but seeing them being crunched up and on their way to the landfill made me feel good. Slowing the assembly line gave me a sense of power over the company.

"About a week later, while I was going over some procurement orders (I'm supposed to immediately review, initial, and transmit the orders to the warehouse for a regular shipment of chip bags) . . . well, I 'accidentally' spilled coffee on the forms. Now, they're at the bottom of my 'in' basket. They're drying. Maybe they might even get lost."

Connie now feels power and a sense of control. The action she has taken for revenge may pass. Or she may go further: close down the line, take her frustration out on the crew under her supervision, or worse. Connie is an employee out of control.

Don't Lead With Your Feelings

How would you have reacted in this situation? Would you have sabotaged one of the potato-chip ovens in order to slow production? Slashed the boss's tires? Quit on the spot, destroying records or equipment? Or would you have ignored the problem but soothed your churning insides with antacids, alcohol, or drugs? Would your family have suffered your irritability, temper, and general distress? Does job stress attack you in the form of ulcers, backaches, migraines, or depression?

Quite often retaliation for loss of control and being made to feel like a pawn is registered in subtle ways, such as Connie's "losing" the procurement forms. The results of revenge rob the company of profits as well as take away an employee's personal self-respect. The extremes of Connie's reaction are a measure of the emotional distress she was feeling.

You are not alone. Remember, resentment, unchecked vengeance, and retaliation cost American companies in overhead that is passed on both to the employee and the consumer. Health-care expenses can reduce net profits by as much as 50 percent. That price tag affects us all right in the wallet. As consumers, we pay higher prices for every product from insurance to detergent because of this sense of powerlessness and lack of perceived choices to deal with workplace negativity, and because we are not getting on with the job.

We're not going to tell you to give up, be trampled, to keep smiling when your workplace is crumbling. We understand that feeling of impending danger, the hostility, the resentment and frustration of not knowing what will happen tomorrow. We're not going to tell you to go back to school, get your degree, color another parachute, and thumb your nose at the old boss when you are accepted as a mover and shaker for a large competitor. But we will help you to focus on your own self-esteem, health, and emotional well-being, in order to take control of what you legitimately can control.

It is this utter loss of personal control that invokes workers to strike out through crime, from petty theft to sabotage of extensive computer systems, or self-sabotage. It's deprivation of being valued as a worker, feeling insignificant, that pushes some workers to lie, telephone their friends halfway across the continent, take home those sticky yellow notepads, sneak out for two-hour lunches, steal time—or turn inward, stealing their own good health. Yet, Connie's boss has a boss also. He too may feel as you do. The ripple effect is taking its toll.

We label our feelings as frustration, anger, resentment, and fear. We try to get even or fight back against "the system." Health costs soar. Consumers eventually see it as increased prices. Therefore, revenge and anger in the workplace eventually affects everyone. But the *one* you're concerned with is you! The feelings Janice, Connie, Theresa, and Vic have experienced happen to most workers at one time or another. You are not alone. Other employees are having the same emotions and similar responses. Perhaps, like you, they feel there are no choices, no options. In addition, do you realize that your boss may also endure those same emotions—the same anger, the same frustration, the same feeling of being undervalued, the same malice toward his or her boss?

Consider the personal price if you choose not to identify with your feelings? In the narratives, we saw how Theresa became hopeless. Vic lost not only his self-esteem but an entire lifestyle. Janice felt humiliated, and Connie compromised her personal values. All of them suffered severe stress reactions.

You have your own story—and your own stress level. Like others in today's workforce, you might become a statistic as benefits in worker's compensation payments exceed the $150 billion per year figure. Or you can make some choices. Your situation may not be just like those described in this chapter, yet, there are probably similarities. Look for those. Then, make a consistent effort to use the techniques outlined. Actually write down your responses—don't just *think* them. As you progress you'll find you can successfully plan a strategy that works. You can gradually take control of your own behavior, take advantage of opportunities, and move toward accomplishing your goal, becoming more effective, more confident, and more of the satisfied and productive person that is truly you.

At the end of each chapter we have listed the three Rs. Just as "readin', 'ritin', and 'rithmetic" are the basics of an education, the three Rs—recognize, respond, and reinforce—will form the basis of an action plan for you.

Recognize

Recognize *what* you want to change in your job situation. Theresa wanted her job to change back to the way it was. Vic wanted the market to change. Janice wanted recognition and validation of her creative efforts. Connie wanted a return to her old job. Each employee wanted to change something that was impossible to change. List what you recognize as the problems in your job. Don't limit these to things that you can change. Brainstorm! Get it all out (examples: workload, company policies, office politics). Use the following questions as guidelines:

1. Write down everything you feel your boss (management) has done to harm you.
2. Write down all the things you feel you do for your boss that go unrecognized.
3. Write down how you feel when the boss reprimands, corrects, ignores you. Do you feel angry, petulant, self-righteous?
4. Write down how you react when those things happen.

Respond

Respond now to the items you have listed. In this chapter, Theresa had control over her attitude. Initially, she saw herself as limited to two choices, quitting or taking the new schedule and responsibilities. By opening herself up to other possibilities, she could see more choices. She could have increased her job skills through courses and schooling, sought positive evaluations from current clients, or built her resumé—not just of jobs held, but of job skills. Then, she might have felt more in control of the situation. Vic could reevaluate his philosophy of workaholism as the way to success in the workplace. Each example given has more options for control than the employee may be able to see. Respond to those things *you* can change and list them here (examples: attitude, job skills, career choices).

Use the following questions as guidelines:

1. Am I receiving value from making the boss wrong? (I'm good and the boss is bad.)
2. What is my reward for telling my tale of woe to friends and coworkers? (Sympathy, understanding, attention.)
3. Am I willing to look at my life in a fresh, more positive way?
4. Are all my facts accurate concerning the boss's alleged wrongdoing?

Reinforce

Now you develop steps to *reinforce* the behaviors you need to change in order to take control. What "next steps" are you willing to take? Here are some "next steps" in our stories.

Theresa committed to taking a short course offered by her church on developing affirmations and positive attitudes. This will reinforce her acceptance, as a first step. Vic not only began an exercise program but also joined a networking group of sales and marketing people with whom he felt he had good rapport and could be understood. This reinforces his commitment to take control of himself and make some changes. Janice decided to confront the CFO in order to let him know her feelings and seek a reconsideration of her very serious proposal. She also had begun a "no send" letter—one she never intended to mail. It outlined her feelings to the CFO. She was seeking to reinforce, to create a new context in which her humiliation had taken place. She decided to view him as an understanding person who simply mis-understood in one situation. Good people can say stupid things.

List the reinforcement actions steps you might want to take. Use these affirmations to get you started:

1. I chose this job.
2. I take responsibility for my actions and feelings.
3. Two positive ways to react when I get annoyed on the job are _____ and _____. (Focus on the task at hand, breathe deeply for a few minutes, get a drink of water.)

TWO

I'm OK—You're Not!

"My first message is: Listen, listen, listen . . . to the people who do the work."

H. ROSS PEROT

Frequently employees, when asked about the causes of on-the-job problems and dissatisfaction, say, "I love my job. I'm a good employee. Management is the problem." The answer begins with blame. According to the employees' point of view, management does not care about their personal goals, desires, needs, and wants. This feeling of being unappreciated increases frustration. Management becomes the target for anger. The "boss" may be the direct supervisor or merely an illusion; an unnamed corporate head that is perceived as controlling your very existence even down to getting a drink of water or using the bathroom.

If you see the workplace as a battleground and picture yourself as a soldier in the trenches, you are not alone. Listen to these statements made by real workers just like you.

Dustin, employed in a large hospital, relates her experience. "When the rumors about merger and layoffs began, we all began looking at each other as though we were enemies. I was reminded of something I read about Vietnam. Soldiers tried not to make friends with new replacements because they might be quickly killed. This may sound dramatic, but I didn't want to see my friends get laid off, but the truth was, better them than me."

Another employee describes the effects of budget cuts. "It was like a medieval siege. We were so short on supplies, we all began hiding and stockpiling. I made a joke one day about an 'internal black market' so we could get our work done, and no one laughed."

CONTROL AND POWER

Control is an important concept in dealing with any situation in which a person feels real or perceived domination, threat, or intimidation by another. Yet, domination and intimidation are inherent in the workplace. According to the dictionary, control is "to have power over someone." Words like guide, restrain, regulate are used as synonyms.

"Well," you say, "there's no news in that headline! The workplace certainly has lots of power over me. My boss, the owners, the stockholders, the people under me consume my time. The people over me want all my energy. Everyone seems to have more control than I do."

Let's try to develop a more practical view of control as affecting those around us. Control is increased by increasing influence and by increasing our feelings of control. And, much of what we perceive as controlling us—bosses, money, the economy—is not quite so black and white. While the boss controls us, she too feels controlled. The boss is susceptible to influence, to control. But do we really consider our *own* ability to influence these forces—to increase our real or perceived influence?

HOW DID I GET INTO THIS?

An important component of increasing control is to change our perception. Perception is reality. If we feel controlled, we are. If we perceive a situation in a certain way, that becomes reality for us. Our perception can be changed by events. Keep in mind philosopher Reinhold Neibuhr's wisdom in the Serenity Prayer.

Grant me the serenity to accept the things I cannot
   change
The courage to change the things I can
And the wisdom to know the difference.

HELL WEEK OR HALLOWEEN

Recently we listened to an employee describing a stressful challenge she was anticipating. Serrila had just joined a corporation as a sales rep with a six-month probationary period for new employees. The company had designed a week of what she described as tests, and at the end of that week the new representatives would be "up or out," as she put it. There was tremendous pressure on her to perform. Not only was the workday to be filled with a series of tests, but in the evenings each employee would be on display during the socializing. Serrila had begun to feel anxious and tearful, and experienced nightmares in which coworkers were tortured by uniformed terrorists. She was eating lots of junk food.

Even though this employee, in response to our questioning, reported a good record of performance, her fears had totally altered her perception. She felt completely powerless. She saw herself as a child, being evaluated by teachers and parents with a report card that was dooming her to extraordinary punishment. As we listened to the employee it seemed she was saying, "I need specific suggestions. I need to get my fear under control. I can't deal with this pressure and stress."

The first suggestion we made shocked Serrila. "You need to plan your wardrobe," was the casual response. She looked at us as though *we* belonged on the couch and she should be sitting in the comfortable chair giving advice.

"Plan my wardrobe? That's the last thing I need to worry about!"

"No," came the response. "It is the first thing. You have tremendous control and power over what you wear. Let's begin in an area in which you have control, in which you have expertise, in which you have confidence."

We proceeded to talk about taking charge of those things over which she truly had control, increasing her sense of personal power in order to offset the fear. In reality she did not know what this coming week would be like, and she had a history of success so far. She might not be the best sales rep, but she certainly was not the worst, according to her own admissions and objective evaluations.

Weeks later Serrila called back. She laughingly said, "My red suit was a big hit. You were absolutely right. Not only did I plan my wardrobe, I started exercising. I had put off all my exercising in order to learn the new inventory software. I took time out to exercise, and you were right. I went into 'hell week' feeling confident, powerful, and very organized. I realized too that organization is very important to me. I had felt very disorganized because of all the pressure and the unknown demands. I felt as though I had to prepare for everything, and as a result I was, in effect, preparing for nothing."

She went on, "It was a very rough week but I got through it and I am going to be made a permanent employee. I'm really grateful to you for focusing me in the right direction."

This example shows in a very small, but powerful, way in which an employee was able to refocus fear, resentment, and anger at "them" into action steps resulting in a sense of power and control. The employee had experienced self-empowerment.

FALSE EVIDENCE APPEARING REAL (F.E.A.R.)

Fear creates inaccurate mental pictures of future events, especially around our jobs. We also create expectations: Being an airline pilot is exciting, doing scientific research is dull, and working in a television studio is glamorous. Very often we don't ask enough questions to find out if the facts will meet our expectations or allay our fears. We may start with false assumptions and soon find ourselves frustrated, disillusioned, and resentful. Serrila's description of being overwhelmed by fear, stress, and pressure is an example of *F*alse *E*vidence *A*ppearing *R*eal.

Carlos had been unemployed for several months. He noticed an ad in the local paper that read, "Television studio needs production assistant. Will train." He thought of the glamour surrounding the media and all the celebrities he would meet. He called and arranged an interview for the next day.

Carlos was so overjoyed when he landed the position that he didn't read the fine print on the job description or listen carefully to the interviewer. At 9:00 the next morning, Carlos reported for his first day in the television industry. "So you're the new assistant, welcome aboard. How about running to the cafeteria and grabbing me a cup of coffee?" the producer said. Carlos returned quickly, anxious to get started. "There's a bunch of old posters and pieces of scrap wood in the back room, Carlos. Take them out to the dumpster in the back of the building, then sweep up. You'll find the broom in the closet." Carlos spent the entire day cleaning up and running errands. By Friday he was disillusioned, bored, and looking forward to a weekend off.

While checking out for the day, the producer approached him. "Carlos, we're a little short of staff this weekend. I'd like you to be here tomorrow morning at 8:00." *There go my plans for Saturday*, Carlos thought, *Oh, well, I can use the overtime money.*

One week later, Carlos received his first paycheck. *This can't be right. I know I should have a bigger check than this.* He went to the boss, who explained, "You're on a monthly salary, not an hourly wage. There's no such thing as overtime pay for exempts." Carlos was angry. And, he began to blame himself. He could have been spared the disappointment by finding out just what he was expected to do, how many days a week he was required to work, and how he was to be paid.

What's Your "1020"?

At this point, let's envision two parallel highways, two choices for Carlos. In one direction there is a series of negative reactions. He could quit, continue to be angry and resentful, look for another job, sabotage the employer and himself, and generally work out anger and frustration in ways that would be destructive to him. As an alternative, let's see how Carlos can take control of a difficult situation.

On Monday morning Carlos asked the boss for fifteen minutes during the day to review his duties. The boss tried to put him off, but Carlos was firm. They set up a fifteen-minute time period in the afternoon. Carlos came to this appointment with ten 3×5 cards and began by saying he was nervous and as a result had written down what he wanted to say. He hoped the boss would excuse the notes. The boss seemed slightly bored and eager to move on with the agenda. Though rattled, Carlos held firm.

He started by making a positive statement. "I have really enjoyed this last week. I have learned a lot and am excited about the future. I also realized that I haven't asked enough questions about the job. I didn't realize about the overtime, and the excitement of working in this television station distracted me from the specifics of the job. I understand now that my job is not as glamorous as I thought it might be. But I would like to look forward to more challenging assignments. I wonder if I could spend an hour of my day editing copy in the newsroom. I noticed they need support, and I think that fits in with what you have told me about what our department does."

Carlos's boss actually seemed relieved. The suggestion was appropriate and not what he had expected. He had expected complaints about overtime, about the menial position, or perhaps even threats, anger, tears. Carlos was taking control of a small aspect of the job. He was asking for something that could lead to a goal without alienating the boss and losing the support of a valuable partner in this job. More importantly, Carlos felt in control. He felt he had "won." He felt that he had made up for his own inadequacies in not carefully evaluating the job, in setting up expectations only to be disappointed. Carlos realized that the hour in the newsroom might not produce a new job, a promotion, or greater opportunities. But at the moment he felt empowered. He felt more in control and had the perception of power as opposed to feelings of disappointment, anger, and self-deprecation.

In this story we can see that Carlos has more to learn. He will have to be able to say *no* and to stand up for himself. He is going to have to learn to keep expectations more in line with reality. Most importantly, aligning himself with the boss, and by asking for something reasonable and within his power to grant, Carlos had created a partnership that would be valuable in the future. He had taken control, influencing his boss while changing his own perception of powerlessness.

ASKING FOR HELP

Lynnette is an executive assistant to a vice president in a large medical services corporation. Her primary job description is to provide secretarial support to her boss. In addition she assists four other individuals who head up important projects and are mostly on the road. Three of the people work very well with Lynnette. The fourth, a relatively new marketing specialist, Don, frequently irritates her with interruptions, questions, and petty requests. She said, "He is always asking me to do simple little things that he could more easily do himself."

Lynnette specifically focused on his need to have her fax and copy single pages. "It is more trouble for him to write out the instructions and put it on my desk than to just go and do it himself," she complained, adding angrily, "I can't just tell him to go and do it himself. You'd think he could figure it out. He's smart, he ought to know. Doesn't he realize I have other work to do?"

For Lynnette it was, "I'm okay, you're the problem!" The more she thought about how wrong Don was, the more resentful she became. As her anger began to occupy her thoughts and interfere with her work, Lynnette realized she needed help. She decided to talk with the in-house EAP counselor. The acronym stands for employee assistance program. Does your company have an in-house EAP? If so count yourself fortunate. If not they may have one on retainer. Your human resources department will direct you.

EAP programs are in effect worldwide and are now internationally accepted as a standard part of any benefit program. Most companies nationwide have EAP benefits and currently 97 percent of *Fortune* 500 companies have such programs available to their employees. The EAP provides confidential counseling services to employees and family members whose personal problems negatively affect their work and well-being. The EAP interacts with the workplace, the employee, the community, and the employee assistance profession. Their trained counselors are required to adhere to a strict code of professional conduct beyond the prevailing standards for professional practice, placing the employee's interest above all else. He or she respects confidential business communication from labor and management representatives and will not disclose information without prior consent. The EAP counselor is qualified to provide consultation, assessment, referral, and follow-up services agreed to by the work organization. Most EAPs are administered through the benefits and/or human resources department of a company. If a company does not have such a benefit, encourage the human resources director to look into providing an EAP for the employees and family members.

In addition, the EAP counselor will refer employees and family members to the most cost-effective community resources, taking into consideration the nature and severity of the problem, treatment resources, and availability of health-care benefit coverage. The employee assistance program maintains a focus on alcohol and drug abuse in the workplace. The assessment and referral process recognizes that substance abuse often causes other problems, especially in the family. The EAP will also provide consultation to labor and management representatives on the constructive confrontation technique to help employees whose personal problems are affecting work performance and attendance. Don't wait when you experience problems like Lynette and Carlos. Take advantage of the services provided by the employee assistance program. It will be invaluable to you.

Together, Lynnette and her counselor developed some steps to remedy the situation. She talked to her boss. He suggested she keep a record and then talk to Don's boss. While Lynnette appreciated that he listened to her, the suggestion did not seem like a good one. (She didn't tell her boss that!) She felt like he was putting her off. Now she had enemy number two.

In her next counseling session, it was suggested that Lynnette confront the man directly. "Simply tell him how you feel." Lynnette lowered her eyes. "Well, I have never been very good at direct communication." The counselor said, "Perhaps we could role-play?" They spent the next fifteen minutes rehearsing. Lynnette left the office feeling confident, and it seemed she would confront Don in a positive way, make some suggestions, and resolve the problem.

When Lynnette returned to the counseling office she seemed quite happy and proud of herself. She had *not* used the role-play and she had *not* communicated directly with him! She had created something that was more comfortable for her. "I made a list of things I do to help him, and I made a list of things that he could do to help me. I presented it to him in terms of being partners. I said there were some things he could do to make my job easier and asked him if there was anything I could do for him that I wasn't currently doing. I handed him my list and he looked it over. He looked up smiling and praised me effusively. He said this list was really helpful and he would really pay attention to it and try to add ways that we could help each other. I was thrilled! I didn't have to speak to him directly, but somehow writing this down seemed okay to me."

Indeed it was. Lynnette had taken control and created the impression she was doing more for him when in reality she was going to be doing less. She had taken control over the part of the relationship that she could influence. She had eliminated a hostile situation and felt empowered. Finally, she had allied herself in empowering him. A partnership was created by this confrontation.

BLAMING IS NOT CHANGING

For the first three months of her job in a chiropractic office, Georgia was on probation, as were all new employees. According to company policy, she was to be hired permanently or let go after a trial period of ninety days. Georgia, a gentle, demure young woman, was good with detail. However, she showed little initiative in going beyond the actual assignment, although the work she did with patient records was superb. Unknown to Georgia, the supervisor wanted "more" from her. The months passed. Georgia watched the calendar. She felt her entire life and financial security were hanging on that decision. Worry deteriorated her confidence level even more. She couldn't speak out, and she was terrified to ask about her employment status.

The administrator of the practice realized that regardless of her attention to detail, Georgia would have to leave. They simply needed a more "take-charge" individual. Within a week of the three "official" months of probation, Georgia was released. When she was told, her face paled slightly but she said nothing. They let her go without further explanation. They didn't even tell her that her last week's pay in the doctor's office would be held for twenty days until the paperwork was completed.

At the end of her final work day, Georgia had taken all of the computer floppy disks with the patient records. In her anger and frustration she had gotten even. Timid Georgia had showed them! But had she? What did this malicious act cost her? She was bitter about how badly she had been treated but turned the anger on herself. Georgia had lost control, acting in a manner totally contrary to her values. The chiropractic practice sent her final check immediately, yet she still refused to return the floppy disks. She could not understand her own vindictiveness and still did not speak out. The office didn't realize that keeping her on without telling her the status of her employment would drive her out of control. They dismissed Georgia as unstable, a kook.

The last time we talked with Georgia, she was still feeling angry, tense, depressed, and spiteful. The entire incident ate away at her. What she failed to realize was that she wasn't punishing the chiropractor or her administrative assistant (the office was again running at top speed). She had only inconvenienced her former coworkers, who were forced to clean up her mess and reenter all the patient records. Unlike the employees in the previous stories, Georgia could not see any alternatives to accepting her situation. Too timid to ask for feedback, she also did not confront her own shyness. She did not ask for help or seek to influence the course of her destiny. She saw herself as a victim. And she was.

With Serrila and Lynnette we see employees who have taken what for them are very big steps but which might seem small steps to the reader. They have both exhibited a good focus on the things that they can control. The greatest improvement concerns attitude. As an employee develops a greater sense of control over outward events, a growing sense of inner control will replace stress. As stress is reduced, symptoms of anxiety, depression, fatigue, and sleeplessness will be reduced.

Each of these cases of employee achievement involves an aspect of self-empowerment. Empowerment refers to giving to oneself the control and authority more often given to others.

- Letting go of limiting beliefs.
- Increasing inner resources and self-confidence.
- Directing creative energies to what you *really* want.
- Transforming behavior patterns from self-defeating to self-creating.
- Moving from problem solving to vision creating.

Empowerment creates a strong and positive change in perspective. Thus, our perception of reality can be dramatically altered.

The opposite of empowerment is *depowerment*. This condition is characterized by blaming, negativity, fear, and confusion.

Rate yourself on each pair of characteristics on a scale of 1 to 10, 10 being on the empowering side, 1 being on the depowering side. Read each pair, and rate yourself by filling the blank with a number which corresponds to your feeling about that characteristic. For instance, if I am a big risk taker, a gambler, I might give myself a 9 on number 2. If I take very few risks in my life and always go with the sure thing, I might rate myself a 3 on number 2.

De/Empowering Checklist

Empowering Characteristics		*Depowering Characteristics*
1. display confidence	_____	display little confidence
2. take risks	_____	play it safe
3. take responsibility	_____	am a victim
4. take action	_____	am reactive
5. have tenacity	_____	give up
6. am "power-on"/ enthusiastic	_____	am "shut-down"/low energy
7. am solution oriented	_____	am problem oriented
8. am willing to be wrong	_____	must be right
9. can handle change	_____	am addicted to security
10. examine without judgment	_____	complain without examination
11. am goal directed	_____	am in confusion
12. participate	_____	withdraw
13. am flexible	_____	am rigid
14. play a "bigger game"	_____	am stuck on a plateau
15. face fear	_____	am fear dominated
16. continue my growth	_____	am staying in this place
17. show my humanness	_____	don't need anyone
18. am receptive to new ideas	_____	am narrow minded
19. am accepting	_____	am judgmental
20. am creative	_____	am not creative

21. am self-directed   _____   am floundering or other-directed

22. am flowing   _____   am resisting

23. am willing to change   _____   must be right

24. keep my agreements   _____   break my agreements

25. live in the present   _____   live in the past or future

TOTAL SCORE   _____

Now total your score by adding all the numbers. A perfect empowerment score is 250. If you score 175 or above, you are above average in power and confidence. If you score between 174 and 125, you are more average and able to handle most challenges. If you score below 125, you are a person who feels *depowered*. You lack confidence and are given to victim postures—blaming, negativity, and fear. It's time to set goals for self-improvement.

Looking at the positive and negative traits you have checked, begin to develop goals for behavior change. The following questions will help you begin the plan for change. The questions are carefully selected from research and case studies. Resist the temptation to lightly skip over questions that may seem unimportant. Be assured that each one will have a definite impact on your results. Read over all the questions first, then go back and carefully consider each one before answering.

1. What are some of the behavior changes I would like to make? For example, have I identified my next step up in the company? Do I work toward vision and goals? Am I able to set limits and assert my own needs? Do I like how I interact with my boss and coworkers?

2. Which behavior of those I have rated on the scale, or identified in question one, affects me the most now? For example, I am addicted to security, and that affects my ability to move up in the company. I am too fond of my niche.

3. How do I think my life will be different once I change?
4. Who and what do I think is holding me back? For example, My belief system holds me back. My fear of change, also.
5. Do I have the right to make any change I desire?
6. Which of the changes am I willing to tackle?
7. Am I ready to begin today?
8. Am I using the past as an excuse to stay where I am?

Having assessed your empowering traits, depowering characteristics, and having developed the basic outline for behavior change, you are now ready for the next step.

Water the seeds, not the weeds. The plan for behavior change should focus on the areas of: increasing self-responsibility (reducing victim status); developing self-esteem (reducing self-deprecation); encouraging trust and risk-taking (reducing fear and blame); and cultivating a positive attitude (releasing negative expectations). Give yourself time, but start today.

BLOOM WHERE YOU'RE PLANTED

John Nasbitt, in his internationally successful book, *Megatrends*, makes an interesting comment on roles in the workplace. He states, "What is called for is nothing less than all of us reconceptualizing our roles." If employees conceptualize themselves as powerless, their roles more like pawns than players, then they will indeed feel the powerlessness, the resentment, the frustration, and the discounting that comes with such a role. If, on the other hand, people perceive themselves as able to take control of small things, attempt to influence decisions, change perceptions, then they begin the process of empowerment.

Nasbitt speaks in global terms, examining large corporate empires. The principles are the same for those of us at "mini," not mega, levels of power. Empowerment is a tool to increase the ability to become influencers rather than victims; persuaders rather than pigeons; and "power full" rather than "power less."

Develop your own definition of control relating to your job. To help you along, recall Serrila's story. Serrila had defined control as being made a permanent employee. With help she began to redefine control in terms of those things that she could directly influence. She started with her wardrobe and exercise. As a result, she gained control over her emotions and her anxiety and fear.

Carlos had thought that landing the job meant control. Giving up his illusion of control, he learned that he could influence his boss through cooperation and partnership. Thus, he *felt* in control.

If we continue with Carlos and Serrila, the next step would be a pat on the back. Do this for yourself now. Celebrate your accomplishment. Simply reading this book, interacting with the exercises, and the willingness to look at your part in difficult situations, in the workplace as well as outside, are great beginnings. Acknowledge yourself for taking time to examine your life, your work, and your future.

Recognize

1. List three situations you have experienced recently in which you felt a lack of control. (Examples: "I was asked to work overtime and couldn't say no," or "I wanted help but didn't ask for it.")
2. Now recognize one or more areas that affect your job where you perceive your boss has no control. (Examples: salaries, benefits, vacation policy.)

Respond

1. For each of the situations listed above, put down some empowering responses over which you do have control. (Examples: "I can't tonight, but tomorrow I'm available if you still need me.") List people who might possibly help; role-play asking for help.

Reinforce

To further develop your confidence and skills for empowerment and change, move to the *Reinforce* step of the three Rs. In this chapter, we'd like you to evaluate your capacity to change. Complete the following inventory on coping with change.

CAPACITY FOR CHANGE
YOUR PERSONALIZED SUCCESS INVENTORY
HOW YOU DEALT WITH CHANGES IN THE PAST

Take at least twenty minutes to complete this exercise, by yourself, or to make the exercise even more effective, discuss the examples with your significant other or a close friend. Better yet, complete the exercise alone and then ask another to rate you. How do the responses differ?

In the past, whether you were aware of it or not at the time, every change you have gone through has been a process that (a) you handled well or felt in control of, (b) you handled adequately or felt somewhat in control of, or (c) you handled poorly or felt you had no control over. As you complete the following items, visualize experiences from the past, and rate yourself on how well you feel you have dealt with each of those changes.

For example, rate yourself as follows:

W = Well (high control)
A = Adequately (some control)
P = Poorly (little or no control)
N/A = Not applicable (did not encounter)

Circle the response that fits you.

1. Leaving home   W   A   P   N/A
2. Suffering the loss of a loved one   W   A   P   N/A
3. Changing jobs   W   A   P   N/A
4. Gaining or losing weight   W   A   P   N/A
5. A breakup in a relationship   W   A   P   N/A
6. Entering a new relationship   W   A   P   N/A

7.	Moving to a new city	W	A	P	N/A
8.	Having children	W	A	P	N/A
9.	Being laid off or fired	W	A	P	N/A
10.	An increase in stress in your life	W	A	P	N/A
11.	Having someone leave you	W	A	P	N/A
12.	Getting a promotion	W	A	P	N/A
13.	Taking on a major new responsibility	W	A	P	N/A
14.	Getting married	W	A	P	N/A
15.	Getting divorced	W	A	P	N/A
16.	Ending or changing a destructive relationship	W	A	P	N/A
17.	Starting a new career	W	A	P	N/A
18.	Graduating	W	A	P	N/A
19.	Learning an important new ability or skill	W	A	P	N/A
20.	Starting a new business	W	A	P	N/A
21.	Being sick or in the hospital	W	A	P	N/A
22.	Having to deal with alcohol or drugs (self)	W	A	P	N/A
23.	Having to deal with alcohol or drugs (other)	W	A	P	N/A
24.	Going to work instead of staying home	W	A	P	N/A
25.	Staying home instead of going to work	W	A	P	N/A
26.	An unexpected financial setback	W	A	P	N/A
27.	Having the kids leave home	W	A	P	N/A
28.	Going back to school as an adult	W	A	P	N/A
29.	Living with war or the fear of war	W	A	P	N/A
30.	A change in faith or religion	W	A	P	N/A
31.	A change in the membership of your household or family	W	A	P	N/A
32.	Losing something of great importance to you	W	A	P	N/A
33.	An unexpected calamity or catastrophe	W	A	P	N/A
34.	A change in the health of someone close to you	W	A	P	N/A
35.	Achieving an important goal	W	A	P	N/A
36.	Setting an important new goal	W	A	P	N/A

TOTALS __ __ __ __

Your Pattern of Dealing With Change

To determine your personal pattern of dealing with change, and to get a clear picture of where you stand now, go back to the first exercise and add up your responses in each of the first three categories. Enter the totals below.

(1) Well　　　　＿＿＿＿

(2) Adequately　＿＿＿＿

(3) Poorly　　　＿＿＿＿

To tell you more about your individual response, add your scores again on these items as grouped:

#1, 4, 10, 21, 22　Well ＿＿＿　Adequately ＿＿＿　Poorly ＿＿＿
28, and 29
(The above questions relate to your feelings and fears.)

#2, 5, 6, 11,　　Well ＿＿＿　Adequately ＿＿＿　Poorly ＿＿＿
16, 23, and 36
(The above questions are about relationships and significant others.)

#3, 9, 12, 17,　　Well ＿＿＿　Adequately ＿＿＿　Poorly ＿＿＿
18, 20, 24, 27
(The above questions relate to job and/or school.)

#7, 13, 19, 25,　　Well ＿＿＿　Adequately ＿＿＿　Poorly ＿＿＿
32, 33, 34, 35, and 36
(The above questions relate to challenge.)

#8, 14, 15, 26,　　Well ＿＿＿　Adequately ＿＿＿　Poorly ＿＿＿
30, and 31
(The above questions are about family.)

The weighting of these areas are around 20 percent each (14–25 percent). Do you see that one or two areas are easier or harder for you to handle when change affects them? For example, some people handle job and challenge better than relationships. By more discretely analyzing your responses, behaviors you wish to modify for the future become more clear.

THREE

Bosses Need Love Too!

"Once in a while there's wisdom in recognizing that the Boss is."

MALCOLM FORBES

The habits, workstyle, and personality of the boss or supervisor influence your attitude and work performance. Do you work for Darth Vadar or Yoda? Probably neither. More likely your boss faces many of the same problems that you do. After all, the person that controls your daily activities and enforces policies and procedures is human too! Saddled with the responsibilities of making decisions, keeping work on track, and trying to please both the person up the "food chain" as well as the employees below, is a real juggling act. How can you expect to win if you don't know what makes the boss tick? Why does she behave the way she does and what's behind her decision making?

THE IMPORTANCE OF UNDERSTANDING YOUR COMPANY

You may never have the desire to be the manager or CEO. But would you like your job to be less confusing and more satisfying? Would you like to know why your boss does what he does? If your answer is yes, read on. Begin now to inform yourself about what the other side is up to. Your boss knows the answers to these questions. What would it be like to know:

1. Why you work as a team instead of alone?
2. Why doesn't management ask your opinion on how your department can be improved?
3. Who will be released first when downsizing occurs?
4. What's the purpose of staggered work hours?
5. What's the real purpose of your evaluation form?
6. What's the reason for new policies on alcohol and drug problems in the workplace?
7. What is a "ten-year workforce protection?"

Where do you find the answers? Your first step would be to read your company's policy and procedures manual. If there isn't one you may suggest the company put one together. Volunteer to help. Go to the library and take out several books about management. There are hundreds available. Great companies share. Just start with a title that sounds interesting to you. In most of these books you will find the plans management has in store for you. You'll find training guides and learn to determine workers' personality types along with ways to provide the best possible working conditions. Some of the most interesting subjects in management books are about communication. Who wouldn't benefit from learning how to interact with a troubled employee and solving office problems? Countless books tell managers how to dress and improve their appearance and how to conduct staff meetings. The information goes on, page after page, book after book. If the books are really about you and your future, doesn't it make sense to read as many as possible?

Our research shows that employees who have a basic desire to learn more about their business environment really excel after attending management workshops, seminars, and lectures. There are hundreds available nationwide. And many are free or cost little. Look in your Sunday paper to find where they are and attend them. Call the chamber of commerce in your city for dates, times, and costs. You may even be able to attend one or two with your boss if you are willing to ask. Will I be able to attend if I'm not a manager or trainee? Of course!

THE IMPORTANCE OF UNDERSTANDING YOUR BOSS

You'll find that seminars have quite diverse subject matter. Yet, almost all include some form of "Boss Typecasting." We'll do our version for you, with an outline of six prominent management profiles and some pointers to help you interact with each type of boss.

The Steamroller

The Steamroller is the boss who frequently interrupts you. His motto seems to be, "Do what I say. Be seen but not heard!" He gives orders and commands, doesn't listen, and expects you to read his mind. To make headway with his style you need to:

1. Stand your ground. You may have to jump at openings, and repeat, but don't back down.
2. Get his attention. Start with a positive statement. Ask for advice or input. Not "help."
3. Make an appointment and meet on his turf.
4. Be organized and logical, using facts.
5. Eliminate small talk and be brief. Cut to the chase. Don't tell a story.

Big Sister (Brother)

Then there's the *Big Sister*. She wants to be your buddy, share personal stories about her family and social life. She may share office gossip but rejects your overtures to familiarity. She'll waste your time and then make demands. With her you need to:

1. Remind her of your priorities. Ask if she'd like to change work assignments.
2. Acknowledge her chitchat and change the subject back to work tasks. Keep a businesslike demeanor.
3. Don't ask personal questions. Rather, say, "How can I help you?"

4. Be flexible but maintain the structure of your workday. For example, the employee might say, "I do want to hear this story, and I have to leave in five minutes."
5. Focus on work issues. Continue to work when she approaches your desk.

The Workaholic

When your boss is a *Workaholic*, she expects you be one too and asks for "voluntary" overtime. She wants you to work over and above your job description. She has high expectations that are hard to live up to. To keep her from making you into a workaholic too, you'll have to:

1. Set up boundaries. Have prepared responses to requests for overtime and favors. For example, "I'd really like to help you and that won't work for me."
2. Work at your own pace. Smile and say, "No."
3. Refuse to be intimidated.
4. Clarify your specific duties and hours with your boss. Perhaps you need to rewrite your job description for her approval.
5. Be patient and don't let the workaholic's habits become yours.

Mr. Flake

Then there's *Mr. Flake*, the absentminded boss. He forgets things, loses files, and papers, can't remember what directions were given so contradictions are frequent. Like the Steamroller, he expects you to read minds. You need to:

1. Acknowledge by repeating the directions.
2. Ask specific questions and set deadlines, even daily times, for completion. "I can start that on Tuesday after 2:00 P.M."
3. Make extra copies of memos.
4. Make a note of all directions.
5. Be clear on your area of responsibilities. A current job description and daily goals can help.

The Shadow

When your boss is *The Shadow*, you'll rarely see her. She disappears and expects you to do everything. She offers few guidelines, and you may not know what is expected of you. You're always guessing, yet you are still held responsible. And she may even make you the scapegoat. You need to:

1. Arrange regular meetings. Keep rescheduling if she cancels.
2. Ask for directions and leave written questions, if necessary.
3. Don't assume and don't cover for her with others.
4. Pin her down as to time of return and what to tell callers.
5. Write it down!

The Quiet Man

When your boss is *The Quiet Man*, he says little and seems evasive. He seldom allows any feelings to show and seems aloof, but is probably shy and insecure. With him you must:

1. Ask open-ended questions.
2. Wait calmly for his reply. Don't fill the silence.
3. Avoid rushing.
4. Don't take his lack of communication personally. Plan enough time to wait.

DEALING WITH STEAMROLLERS

Aaron explains his experience when he became the unsuspecting victim of a Steamroller's management style. "I was hired as a revenue officer for the Federal Bureau of Investigation in Fresno, California. During my first five years I received numerous special details including manager in San Francisco. Four years later, I was promoted to a group manager position in Denver, Colorado. During my career with the FBI, I have received many Special Act and Superior Performance awards, including the coveted Outstanding Manager award. I have found my years with the service to be both demanding and rewarding. I say this to explain that I'm both experienced and pretty successful. Yet I found myself in a 'boss' dilemma.

"Undoubtably, my most difficult time as a manager was while I worked for Barbara. Barbara was a few years younger than me. She was my division chief and managed six group managers, like me. At the time she became my boss, I had already established myself as a respected frontline manager. I was supportive of my employees and succeeded in promoting several into management. On the other hand, I didn't hesitate to pursue performance problems when appropriate. Before Barbara's arrival, I had taken on several hard-core problems in the office but still maintained the respect of the employees and the union. My group's productivity and quality of work was always equal to or better than the norm. I had received performance awards each year.

"In the face of all this, Barbara seemed intent on destroying me. As my division chief, she was my immediate supervisor. She was openly hostile to me, critical of most everything I did. In her reviews of my group, she focused on the few deficiencies, while ignoring the positive aspects. (It's very easy to find the problem areas if that's what you want to find.) She emphasized the substandard work being done by one of my employees without recognizing my efforts to correct the problem. Barbara belittled me and seemed to relish being my 'superior.' She made sure I knew who was the boss. I recall once we were trying to coordinate a meeting, and I suggested to Barbara that she tell me where she was going to be on a certain day so I could contact her. She literally shouted at me, 'I'll be damned if I'm going to tell some group manager where I am going to be!'

"Barbara continued her efforts to knock me down. In one of her discussions, she told me I should just 'cut my losses' by stepping down from management. My attempts to dissuade her were ignored. I took my case to her boss, the chief. I pointed out how unreasonable and inconsistent Barbara had been. He listened patiently, but not surprisingly, backed Barbara (the chief is the same person who had previously approved my annual performance awards.)

"Barbara suffered severe mood swings," Aaron continued. "She could be pleasant on occasion and a real bitch at another time. It seemed Barbara had to prove she was better than everyone else, especially men. She frequently held discussions standing in front of my desk, instead of sitting at my level. I believe she thought taking me down would be a real feather in her cap. After months of her constant rankling, Barbara began to wear me down physically and mentally. My self-confidence was undermined, and I began to question my own abilities. I felt powerless. To make things worse, the employee union somehow got a copy of the proposed management removal letter. Word quickly got around that I was about to be dumped from management. I was embarrassed and humiliated. I considered legal action against the union.

"Fortunately, I received tremendous support from my family, particularly my wife. She helped me through the crisis. Without her, I would have been mentally crippled from the experience. Eventually I transferred to another division. I did the only thing I could have. I got out from under Barbara's control before she succeeded in destroying me. I look back on this experience and wonder, how did someone like Barbara ever get into such a position of power? I heard later that she had a somewhat checkered career before becoming a division chief. Just how did she get advanced to middle management? I still ponder this question."

After his transfer, Aaron went on to reestablish his reputation. Two years later, he was selected as "outstanding manager" of his division and was subsequently promoted to division chief. The Steamroller had not been successful in her attempts to destroy Aaron. He rose above her onslaught, made a positive choice, and succeeded. He did not seek revenge. He knew who and what his challenges were and responded in a professional manner. At times we get through each day the best we can until the situation is resolved.

WHERE IS THE SHADOW?

Terri had been the office manager in charge of thirty-three employees for several years. Mr. Angelo was the owner and out of the office most of the time. He always seemed to be with clients, either at their sites or entertaining them at lunch or dinner.

This boss was the Shadow. Terri enjoyed her job but wished Mr. Angelo would come in more often or at least keep in contact with her during the day. She never knew when he would show up. When he did, his voice came through the door before he did. "Where is everybody? What do I pay you people for? Terri!" he shouted, "Get me the Kincaid plans in my office, NOW!" She hurried to his office and handed him the file. "These aren't the plans I wanted! Can't you do anything right? I told you last week I would need the updated printout." Terri knew he had not told her about the plans, but said nothing. "Get the design team in here now, we're going to have a little chat!"

The team filed into Mr. Angelo's office. After they were seated Mr. Angelo stood up and began to pace. "You people have let me down again. Why can't you get it together? You have had a week to come up with the Kincaid plans." A wave of protest came from the team. "We didn't know . . . nobody told us!"

"Terri," Angelo said, "How could you slip up like this? You've made a costly mistake."

Good Lord, he's done it again, Terri thought. *He goofs up and I'm the scapegoat.* Terri glanced around the room. The team stared at her. Some shuffled their feet. She heard herself say, "I'm sorry, I must have forgotten."

After the meeting Terri went to Mr. Angelo's office. It was time for a talk. First she explained how much she enjoyed working for the company. Then she told him she would no longer take the blame for something she didn't do and that she would like to meet with him weekly. She asked that he also provide her with a "to do" list instead of verbal communication. Terri felt good when she left the office. It was a start. Mr. Angelo was not a bad person; it was his way of behaving that was irritating. Terri was wise enough to know that it's the act, not the person, that is deplorable.

UNDERSTANDING THE WORKAHOLIC

Frankie is an entrepreneur, the owner and operator of a small manufacturing company. He has an extraordinary need for control. He came up the hard way, with a limited formal education. He is self-taught and proud of it. The company is his baby. At forty-one years old, he is in great physical shape, swimming daily in his pool and working out in his home gym. He is an enthusiastic "people person" with enough desire and ambition to make up for his lack of schooling.

It is well known that Frankie can charm the socks off the toughest customer. They would come in complaining and leave laughing at one of Frankie's stories. But Frankie creates a lot of confusion around him that is unsettling for his employees. He finds himself outdistancing the others. He's always pushing. The further ahead he gets, the greater his efforts to pull his team along. He thinks they're holding him back. Frankie's solution to his problem is to harass, bully, cajole, flatter, yell, and when all else fails, promise what it takes to keep his "baby" moving.

Frankie brings in last-minute orders on a regular basis and demands his employees work excessive overtime to meet unrealistic deadlines. He is everywhere! He wants to be involved everywhere, from the mail room to the art department to the warehouse. He's often countermanding the foreman's orders to the crew. He creates havoc, changes plans that have been in the works for months, then expects employees to work on their day off to bring the project up to speed. When one of his warehouse workers recently asked if he could go home after a twelve-hour shift, Frankie humiliated him by saying, "Can't take the heat, can you? Maybe I should hire a couple of cheerleaders to take your place." Frankie likes to take advantage of such a situation to tell his story to the workers. Did they know he

slept only four hours at night? Did they know that he spent
most of the night on the phone with his suppliers in Ireland and
that he built this company from nothing . . . with help from no
one? Frankie can work seven days a week for several months,
then fly to Ireland to visit his suppliers. But only his body
leaves the office. All day the faxes and overseas calls come to
the office.

A young receptionist went to him once saying she couldn't
work late because she had a class to attend. He fired her. She
left in tears. Frankie called her the next day and rehired her.
When she returned to work, there were two dozen roses on her
desk. She went to the office and thanked him. He responded by
telling her she had to get with it, that hard work was good for
her and would make her sharp. Frankie alluded that there would
be some hefty Christmas bonuses this year for people who went
the extra mile. It was typical of Frankie to attack his workers
with unreasonable demands one minute and reward them the
next. Once, after a particularly rough staff meeting filled with
name-calling and blame, Frankie invited the entire staff to dinner
at a very expensive restaurant, and he picked up the tab. At the
dinner he was charming, laughing, making jokes. All the anger
and frustration melted away as he told them what a great team
they were. He told them that they would be stockholders when
the company went public. Frankie was a dynamo dream-spin-
ner. While he was speaking with them, his cellular phone was
in hand. Frankie never stopped. The next day was chaos as
usual.

As you might imagine, this company experiences high
turnover. Within one year, three sales managers quit. Over a
dozen warehouse workers and office personnel were either ter-
minated or quit. The remainder of the crew discussed setting up
a meeting with Frankie. They liked him, in spite of his "craziness," and could see the damage Frankie was causing. The meeting was held on-site. Frankie set the time at six in the morning.
The group had invited a special guest to join them. It was Mr.
Lopez, a member of the board of directors for the company, who

would act as spokesman for the employees. Frankie commented that it looked like a lynch mob.

"Not so," said Mr. Lopez. "Our purpose this morning is to create a win-win situation. Frankie, your employees like you. They are experienced, bright people who want this company to succeed. We are all of the opinion that you have the earmarks of a workaholic, and that's fine . . . for you. We are not asking that you change who you are. What we do ask is that you don't ask us to be the same."

Frankie interrupted, "I don't understand what all the resistance is about. Can't they just follow orders and do the job? That's what I pay them for. They need to rev up their production and make fewer mistakes. I have to see that they do. Business is business. If this company goes down there won't be any jobs to gripe about."

Mr. Lopez heard him out. "Frankie, we are aware that you own this company, you are the boss, you call the shots. The difficulty is the manner in which you behave. In other words, it's not what you say, it's how you say it. You also have a tremendous amount of energy. Physically, most of us do not have your drive. Your sole focus is on the company and taking it to the top. That's okay. On the other side, you have employees with families; they deserve to spend time with them. You have young mothers who must pick up their children from sitters after work. They have a life outside of the company."

Frankie spoke. "I try to give you people a good place to work. Look at some of the great parties we've had. I also pay a hell of a lot of money for your health-care benefits." Frankie's feelings were hurt. Mr. Lopez said to think about some possible solutions before the next meeting.

During the following week, Frankie stayed out of the building. Mr. Lopez was in charge. It was a breath of fresh air. The work was done, and with few mistakes. No yelling, no panic. The employees missed Frankie's motivation and humor, but not his aggressive style. The next meeting had a different tone. Frankie was his smiling self and Mr. Lopez smiled too. The announcement made by Frankie was a shocker.

"Look folks, I told you that I'm not going to change. I like to be on the fast track and see results. That's who I am. I see the vision, and it has upset me that you people don't. This is my decision, based on Mr. Lopez advice. I'm bringing in a business psychologist to work with all of us. Mr. Lopez tells me they have been of great benefit to many companies and the results are often positive. We'll see." The employees had stood their ground with Frankie; they were not intimidated.

REGAIN THE JOY IN THE JOB

Make a list of things in your job that give you (or used to) joy, satisfaction, happiness, or elation. Visualize specifics and reflect on the tasks for a moment. Now, create your own affirmations and write, say, and read them daily with real feeling. Affirmations spoken in a hopeless or sarcastic tone are less effective than those issued forth with meaning and force.

Replace	*With*
My boss is so disorganized.	My boss is extremely efficient.
My boss is grouchy.	My boss likes to joke around. I can encourage this behavior by smiling.
My boss ignores me.	My boss is a busy man. He takes time for me if I need it, and I can learn to speak up.
My boss won't give me a raise.	My boss is reasonable. If I prove myself, I will be rewarded.
My boss hates me.	My boss doesn't know me well. If I take time to let her know me, intimacy will come.
My boss picks on me.	My boss is detail-oriented. I can learn from her to be more precise and accurate.

By placing the behaviors in a different context—putting a different frame on the picture—you can focus more on yourself, reducing time spent on blaming and procrastination.

SETTING BOUNDARIES

One point must be made about the line between setting boundaries and taking abuse. If your employer is being verbally abusive or harassing you in any way, you should immediately contact your employee assistance program representative or human resources department. They will help you assess an abusive situation. Even though the boss's behavior may have been tolerated by others, there are channels and procedures to support you.

Jean took a new job as support secretary for a real estate firm. She quickly realized that her main boss was out in the field most of the time and was unavailable to her when he was in town. As support person for nine sales reps, she found herself swamped with unreasonable demands, rude behavior, and frequent requests to work through lunch and overtime. Jean realized that the person who had previously occupied the position had obviously set few boundaries, created no structure, and was pretty much a doormat for the group of agents who considered her their gofer.

Without any clear guidelines from her boss, Jean felt she was on her own. She researched setting boundaries by rereading some books on codependency. Slowly she started establishing boundaries on the job. She sent out a memo letting the agents know that sell sheets needed for weekend open houses would have to be submitted by 3:00 P.M. on Thursday. She attached an easy-to-use form she had created, which simplified the process and made clear what she needed. This solved the problem she had been having of last-minute Friday deadlines and having to stay late to make copies. She was fairly lenient during the grace period as the agents became used to her new system, but she eventually let certain agents know that they could make their own copies if they turned in their material late.

She began to create structure around the office, which made her boss happier, her coworkers happier, and pleased her. The office began to seem less hurried, hectic, and crazy. As a fringe benefit, Jean later asked her boss if the company would pay for her to go to school for a real estate license. He agreed to subsidize her classes at community college and to pay for her test. When she received a license, her value to the company increased.

Jean learned to set limits, and get what she could out of her job. She was willing to devote some time and effort into turning the position around. You too can turn your position around. Make your job what you want it to be. Don't be afraid to ask for what you want, especially in the way of fringe benefits. For example, a bonus for a special project that increases revenue. Or compensatory time for working long hours or holidays. Remind yourself of those fringe benefits that add value to your job when problems do arise.

Jean supported more than one boss, and in this day of cutbacks, layoffs, and downsizing, many of you will be providing support for multiple bosses, or even an entire department or company. You may get along fine with most of the people you work with, but sometimes there is that one person you simply don't get along with. If that person is a boss or manager, it becomes more difficult. Be it a personality conflict, differences in workstyle, or whatever; you don't like her, and she doesn't like you.

There are some strategies for working with that one person you can't get along with. Keep a log of all communications with that individual. Quite often miscommunications can be the source of interpersonal difficulties, and clearing the lines can solve that problem. Get clear with this person and stay clear. When asked to do something, restate the request as you understand it. "So, you are asking me to call John back to confirm your appointment?" Make sure you are clear. Vagueness and uncertainty will only work in someone else's favor. When you are clear, you are in control. When you are unclear or are given unclear directions, you give up control. Admitting you don't understand helps you to regain control of a situation. Call the person back if you need to and say, "I'm really not clear on what it is you wanted me to do here," and ask for clarification.

WHAT DOES IT ALL MEAN?

Almost every boss has good traits. We hope you can find some in yours. And, every boss surely has some bad traits. Somehow, some days, these seem to overshadow the good ones. With human behavior as complicated as it is, and business pressures what they are today, this is inevitable. No boss, like no job, can be perfect—unlike you, who we hope is the perfect employee.

The characteristics and behaviors we've profiled above may be subtle in your boss. Look for similarities and ignore the differences, so you can focus on action steps. Or maybe you've found others we've barely touched on. The value is in the discovery. So do your homework. Get to know your company, the ownership philosophy, and the personnel dynamics. Keep your eyes and ears open. Be objective. Once you "know the enemy," peace is possible. At least you'll know enough to cope. And you just may become a better business person.

Here are some exercises that might help you understand your boss and how to cope.

Recognize

1. Review everything you feel your boss (management) has done to harm you.
2. Make a list of all the things you feel you do for your boss that go unrecognized.
3. Consider how you feel when the boss reprimands, corrects, ignores you. Do you feel angry, petulant, self-righteous? Be specific about your feelings.

Respond

1. What value do I receive from making the boss wrong? (e.g., I'm good and the boss is bad.)
2. What is my payoff for telling my problems to friends and coworkers? (Sympathy, understanding, attention, etc.)

3. Am I willing to look at my work in a fresh, more positive way? Have I ever done the same thing my boss is doing? Did anyone give me a break?
4. Are all my facts accurate concerning the boss's alleged wrongdoing?

Reinforce

Repeat the following:

1. I chose this job and take responsibility for it.
2. I encourage myself to laugh and see the humor in each day.
3. I reward myself when I deal well with difficulty on the job by _____.
4. Focus on the task at hand, breathe deeply for a few minutes, get a drink of water.
5. Forget about counting to ten. Count to one thousand before saying anything that could make matters worse.
6. Have a forgiving view of people. Believe that most people are doing the best they can.

FOUR

"A Rose By Any Other Name . . ." (Workstyle Personality)

"Knowledge is power." Whoever first said that phrase is right up there with the gal who invented Post-its. The statement is a part of everyday speech. It is an unarguable reality. And yet we often fail to use the route of learning for gaining power. But, you say, "I know my job very well. I have been doing it for a long time. In fact, I have created much of the job that I do." Knowledge of the job alone is not enough.

Our problems are created by our personal interactions with people. When a machine breaks down we experience an inconvenience, creating a problem. But it is the associated problems and reactions of the *people* affected by the breakdown that exacerbate the problem. The machine can be fixed, but harsh words and hurt feelings are generated by people. The memories of anger and hurt and the impaired relationships continue to create resentment. Thus, knowledge about *people*, about *workstyle personalities*, is an important tool for self-empowerment. Learning to better communicate and mesh with different personalities is a critical part of success in the workplace.

Mae-lin, a young, dedicated CPA, worked for a large accounting firm. She had two promotions in her first year on the job, and over the four years she worked for the company, she developed a reputation for attention to detail, flawless work, reliability, and precision. Her problems at work began when she received a promotion to the position of manager of the auditing department. Now she was responsible for others but also had a new boss. As department manager she came under the supervision of Dennis, a bright "comer," who immediately found fault with her. It seemed everything she did was wrong in his eyes. He was annoyed by the amount of time she took to produce reports. He felt she should delegate more responsibility now that she was a manager. He told her that she did not communicate well in senior staff meetings.

Mae-lin tried to listen and incorporate Dennis's comments into her workstyle, but she was afraid to delegate, and when she did so she invariably found errors in the work of her subordinates. Nobody, it seemed, could do the high quality of work that she performed. Mae-lin became more and more frustrated and began, for the first time in four years, to feel inadequate in her job. She felt frustrated by her inability to communicate her problems to Dennis. She also resented that she had received no praise from him, no acknowledgement for the many "correct" things she was doing. She thought of quitting her job, but such an idea created more problems than it solved. Besides, she disliked change. The thought of looking for a new job and all the attendant problems frightened her. She began to experience sleeplessness, anxiety, fatigue, and other signs of depression. Finally she sought the help of an employee-assistance counselor.

Mae-lin was experiencing a crisis in the workplace. The solution to the problems she was experiencing lay in looking at workstyle personality rather than work tasks. Her workstyle personality was characterized by a very analytical approach to work. Precision, attention to detail, follow-through were all personality attributes that had created her very positive reputation in the company. With her promotion to manager, however, something different was required of her. Mae-lin needed to change her workstyle personality. Specifically, she was asked to pay less attention to detail, to be more outgoing and communicative, to lead the team rather than be merely a team player—all characteristics of a more gregarious personality type. She was also experiencing a supervisor with a workstyle personality that was very different from hers. Neither Mae-lin nor her supervisor could perceive their differences in terms of personality, but we can. Let's take a closer look.

For Mae-lin, organization, analysis, perfectionism, and thoroughness were part of the guiding principles of her life. Such a personality type does well with data and technical detail, which accounted for much of her success in the accounting profession. She would have done equally well in medical, scientific, or legal work. Mae-lin was also a loyal employee and very hardworking. But her personality needed support in other areas. She was not a natural leader. She had a tendency to be inflexible and get bogged down by details. She was not good at seeing the big picture or making quick decisions. Until her promotion, all of these missing or negative characteristics had not been a problem. However, as a manager she was required to exhibit more leadership, delegate more work, and accept a style of work that was different from her own and that made her uncomfortable.

Meanwhile, Dennis, her supervisor, exhibited *his* preferred personality style. He judged others by their ability to communicate, to see the big picture, to forego small details, and make quick decisions. He dominated situations in order to overcome obstacles. He expected behaviors like his own personal style in Mae-lin. On the other hand, he needed someone like Mae-lin who was thorough and concerned with detail. Dennis could have learned to appreciate her capacity for loyalty and hard work. But because some of her predominant characteristics were not valued by him he overlooked those aspects of her personality that he did hold in high regard.

Does this mean that Mae-lin can't be a good supervisor? Of course not. Mae-lin and the counselor worked together to accommodate her comfort level and still meet the demands of her position as a manager. Mae-lin learned to prepare notes before each meeting and rehearsed some statements to make on agenda items. She assertively volunteered for committee assignments instead of waiting to be asked. As she spoke in these limited areas, she began to feel more confident and began to speak more freely.

And what about Dennis? Is he just an insensitive jerk? As Maelin changed the way she interacted with Dennis, he praised her comments in the meetings and complimented the E-mail delegation system she had established. Both were modifying their preferred and automatic styles to accommodate the other. They were acting on a modified "golden rule." "Do unto others as they want you to!"

A personality is like a snowflake. It resembles the others in many ways, but no two are identical. Each day your personality in the workplace determines much about what you think and feel and how you behave. It determines how you make decisions; it determines what things are threatening to you. It is a factor in each personal interaction.

Several years ago Patt and I were contemplating a trip to Kenya. I was excited about the trip, looking forward to safariing, photography, and typical tourist pleasures, when suddenly it occurred to me that I might be in some physical danger from the animals. Of course, the closest I had been to a dangerous animal was on the back of a tame horse! As I mulled over the idea of whether or not I might be *afraid*, I mentioned my feelings to Patt. She laughed! I didn't understand why she found what I said so funny.

She smiled and said, "Oh, no! I know what you'll be afraid of."

"What?" I said, "I really want to know."

"*Boredom*," she replied, "You are afraid of being bored!"

As a good friend of many years, Patt knew me very well. And, she was making an intuitive assessment of my workstyle personality, which I was taking on vacation. I was frightened, actually phobic, of being bored. And without knowing it, my fear of boredom had led me to make preparations for entertainment. I was making lists of books to take, packing crossword puzzles, and in fact, I had planned to take office work along. (I was going to keep all this secret from my traveling companions for fear of their ridicule!) But my workstyle personality was pervasive. Boredom was my fear.

Each of us has a distinct workstyle personality. A few of us are aware of what that workstyle personality is, or intuitively make choices that reflect such awareness. We know well the conditions under which we work best. We try to make these conditions a reality. However, like Mae-lin, we find that conditions change and we must adapt and accommodate. We must get out of our "comfort zone" or we will eventually feel powerless and out of control.

Patt tells a story of personality literally on display in the workplace. "I recently walked into the data processing offices of a large insurance company where I had been asked to consult on marketing strategies. The large workroom had just been remodeled and the area was quiet, light, and very conducive to concentration. Each worker had an individual cubicle that was well soundproofed and padded, even though all were open. As I looked across the room I counted about forty cubicles. The sound level was quiet and the environment was pleasant, though seeming to lack individuality. But then my vision was attracted to a few items that stuck up from the tops of the four-foot-tall open cubicles. Some employees had fixed small stuffed animals, cartoon caricatures, flowers, plastic figures, and other small objects on the top and sides of their cubicles. They identified their territory, but even more so, their personalities.

"If you could have a bird's-eye view of these cubicles, you would see how each one reflected the employee's workstyle personality. Some had placed family pictures prominently throughout their cubicles. Pictures of babies, weddings, and themselves with celebrities or at parties predominated. Others had very tidy and immaculate cubicles with no extra clutter on the work surfaces. Others showed humor, displaying cartoons, bumper stickers, and slogan buttons. Still others showed nurturing and caretaking aspects of personality with flowers, candy dishes, and potted plants (and probably a tiny sewing kit in the drawer). Seeing a philodendron tendril lovingly pinned so that it reached the top of the cubicle for as much sunshine as it could get, I thought, *Workstyle personality in action.*"

To gain control and be empowered by your own personality, you must first understand its distinctive nature and learn for yourself how you are like or different from others. There are many ways to learn more about personality. One way is to take a professionally administered individual personality test. Often these tests are used in hiring decisions, administered in training, or used with promotion. If you are interested in an in-depth assessment, talk to an employee assistance counselor, check with the human resources or training department, or look in the yellow pages for testing services. But for our purposes, or for perhaps a first step, let's try something simple.

Take the test on the page opposite to develop an understanding of your personality. People are different, but we are more alike than different. Each one of us is unique and special, yet we share many common personality patterns and styles. The intent of this exercise is not to put you in a box or to stereotype you, but simply to provide an additional dimension of understanding. When you complete the exercise, follow the instructions on page 56 to determine which of the four personality types best describes you. Now you have been labeled!

The Entertainer

Influencing, persuasive, often a talented actor, this personality characterizes Johnny Carson, Ronald Reagan, and Oprah Winfrey. This personality type is warm, creative, charismatic, and energetic. Entertainer types talk a lot, entertain, tell jokes, and generally dominate a conversation. They like to be the center of attention and communicate well. They are people oriented and usually optimistic. They value popularity and social recognition.

These qualities characterize their work and personal styles. Their value to an organization is obvious. In terms of work, the downside often includes a lack of follow-through, self-centeredness, reputation as "flakes," and lack of attention to detail. They

EVALUATE YOUR STYLE

Check the word from each pair that best answers the question, "If I were forced to choose, I would say I am . . ." Choose the one that applies 51 percent of the time or more. Answer all.

I		**II**	
more animated	____	more passive	____
more a leader	____	more a follower	____
more assertive	____	more accepting	____
more challenging	____	more hesitant	____
more lively	____	more meditative	____
more confrontive	____	more supportive	____
more gregarious	____	more a listener	____
more a risk-taker	____	more cautious	____
more intense	____	more relaxed	____
more forceful	____	more tentative	____
		TOTAL	____

Total the check marks in column II and put that score on the TOTAL line. Circle the TOTAL number on the horizontal line on the graph on page 56.

III		**IV**	
more flashy	____	more formal	____
more spontaneous	____	more disciplined	____
more responsive	____	more self-contained	____
more impulsive	____	more methodical	____
more intimate	____	more distant	____
more feeling	____	more analytical	____
more people oriented	____	more task oriented	____
more outgoing	____	more reserved	____
more dramatic	____	more matter-of-fact	____
more warm	____	more cool	____
TOTAL	____		

Total the check marks in column III and put that score on the TOTAL line. Then circle the TOTAL number on the vertical line on the graph below.

					10	Intimate/Warm						
					9							
	Entertainer				8		**Cooperator**					
					7							
					6							
Dominant/Directing	0	1	2	3	4	5	6	7	8	9	10	Casual/Easygoing
					4							
					3							
	Dominator				2		**Precisionist**					
					1							
	Distant/Reserved				0							

may fail to see the important points, letting their desire for social recognition and popularity take precedence.

Cooperator

Agreeable and personable, this type is caring, helpful, and definitely a team player. Cooperators prefer to be supporters rather than leaders. They like harmony, are very likable, loyal, and value security and belonging to a group. Jimmy Carter, Ed McMahon, and Nancy Reagan share these qualities. They are helpful, predictable, and patient. In the workplace, this style contributes to their success. Limitations may be seen in their wish not to take risks, their avoidance of constructive conflict, their inability to be critical or express negative feelings. When thwarted over time they may become resentful and engage in passive aggressive actions.

The Dominator

Not only directing the play, this type wants to be the actor, producer, and critic. Dominators attempt to control and dictate.

They are decisive and direct. They get things done and are good at seeing the "big picture," accomplishing goals, and overcoming obstacles. In the workplace their confidence and decision-making ability is an asset but may be mistaken for arrogance. They are good leaders, businesslike, and task oriented. But for each type there is a shadow side. Directors may become bullies, display insensitivity to needs unlike their own, alienate and intimidate others. Lyndon Johnson, Margaret Thatcher, and Henry Kissinger exhibited this personality style. John F. Kennedy displayed the classic leadership style of dominance coupled with a high level of the Entertainer style.

The Precisionist

Attentive to detail, logically analytic, this type of personality is systematic, consistent, and accurate. Such personality types value facts, data, and precision. They like control, structure, the status quo, and accepted order. They are not known for their communication skills and may flee in the face of controversy, become silent, or alternately autocratic and given to lecturing. Coach Tom Landry, Katharine Hepburn, and George McGovern share these traits. In the workplace these qualities are very desirable, again, given the right position. Security and order are part of each workday for the Precisionist. On the downside they can be stubborn, aloof, and boring. They often move slowly, resist change, and fail to express feelings, especially of a personal nature. They are uncomfortable with intimacy and emotion.

Your style—whether Dominator, Entertainer, Cooperator, or Precisionist—doesn't reflect all your qualities. Each of us has a bit of each style in our makeup. When angry the most gentle Cooperator can act out his rage and throw tantrums. When pressed the Entertainer can make a budget and balance a checkbook. The idea is that we have a preferred or dominant style. These are the attributes that shape your personality most strongly. No personality is one-dimensional. There is no good or bad, no right or wrong. For every person who enjoys being on stage, there is someone in the audience terrified of public speaking. For every person who defines a good job as one that lasts his or her entire working life, there is another person who changes careers as many as seven times in a lifetime. There is no right or wrong, no good or bad, just differences.

Understanding our own personalities helps us to understand and accept the way others work and relate to us in the workplace. All of us harbor certain undeveloped, or perhaps "secret," abilities within our list of attributes. We can often discover in our personalities a larger number of possibilities for our working relationships than we might have suspected. As we begin to use better ways of communicating, we also learn more about others. They in turn reveal "secret" abilities and offer more depth in a relationship than we might have anticipated. The people around us take on new dimensions. The working relationships grow and are more successful.

SUCCESS IS A SYSTEM—NOT ROULETTE

Hank had consulted with us in his capacity as director of marketing for a large casino. He worked in Reno but flew all over the world finding new locations for sites and helping foreign countries establish their own casinos and tourist attractions. His description of the job created visions of glamour, "high rollers," and stacks of roulette chips! Hank, however, was thwarted by the business manager we'll call Mike. Hank, handsome, six-foot-two, straightened his "Countess Mara" tie and flashed a Rolex as his French cuffs slid up. He gestured broadly, saying, "Mike simply doesn't understand what marketing is. He doesn't get that you have to spend money to attract these people. He constantly questions my expense account and budgets. He doesn't understand that high rollers expect to be taken to lunch, to go first class. They expect the limousines to pick them up." Hank became more agitated as he waved his arms and talked faster. "He's always bugging me about petty details. I can't get my budgets approved without him going over it with a fine-toothed comb. He makes me justify everything."

When I asked what Hank had tried in order to effect solutions, he responded, "I've tried everything! I've given him complimentary tickets to ball games and special seats for openings. I had his wife picked up in a limousine for a shopping trip with other VP wives. I have done everything. He doesn't want the tickets. He seems disappointed by all my efforts. I just don't know how to relate to him."

Because this was a workshop in workstyle personality we involved all the members of the group to provide a solution to Hank's problem. We had previously studied workstyle personality and had identified each personality type. The group was asked to begin by identifying Hank's personality even though we knew it well. Hank is definitely an Entertainer, one who influences others, a born persuader. He is perfect as a salesperson, outgoing, entertaining, and likable. He is also a flashy dresser. Each week we could look forward to a new outfit that was both expensive and perfectly suited to him. Members of the group had no trouble in identifying Hank's personality, in pigeon-holing him perfectly! Hank smiled as aspects of his personality were revealed, including negative ones—lack of attention to detail, not wanting to be confined by traditional standards, judging others by action rather than thought. Hank knew that he had these limitations in his personality. He expected others to support him, to pick up the pieces where his "personality" left off.

The group was then asked to paint a personality picture of Hank's nemesis, the chief financial officer, Mike. The group became animated, describing him as a man who wore brown suits, and when his suit coat was removed, he had a plastic pocket protector. He carried sharpened pencils and pens and had worked as an accountant before his promotion to CFO. In general, Mike was described as having an analytical, Precisionist style.

Hank was then asked to bring his chair into the center of our circle and to select from the people in the group the one who had the Precisionist workstyle of his nemesis, the person most like Mike. A little embarrassed, Hank pointed to Janet. She brought her chair to the center of the room. I asked the two of them to role-play how Hank would ask for an increase in his budget, and Janet's job was to act as her personality suggested. Hank stood up and reentered the circle as if entering an office. He remained standing. "Hi there, Janet. I've got two tickets to the new show opening Saturday night at the Luxor. I thought you and your hubby might enjoy it. By the way, I need about a thousand more in my budget for the upcoming golf event. You know we've got some big spenders coming in, and you know they expect the best."

Janet just looked at Hank. Several moments elapsed before she responded. "Thank you," she said slowly, "for the tickets. Do you have a detailed proposal for the budget increase?"

"Oh, come on, Janet," Hank laughed, "You know me. . . . You can fill in all those details. You know how much this stuff costs. What do you want from me?" Hank began to scribble some notes on a piece of paper taken from her desk. "Look, here are the items and here are the amounts we need to increase them by. Is that good enough?" Janet crossed her arms and said that she would take a look. The role-play ended.

Janet seemed to be angry. She was pulling away from Hank and seemed almost resentful of her position. When asked about her feelings, she laughed, "Yes, I did become angry and resentful. I really got into the role. The word that comes to mind for me is *frivolous*. I think Hank is frivolous. He doesn't understand the meaning of money. He doesn't have any respect for my job. He throws these tickets at me, yet he has never once asked me to do anything with him."

This was very interesting. In such a brief, contrived moment Janet's personality was clearly in contrast and in conflict with Hank's. Hank sat very still. It seemed for the first time he had begun to see Mike as a person rather than an obstacle to his desires. We then pursued the feelings that Mike and Janet might have had. The group validated the impression of anger and feeling discounted on Mike's part. We made several suggestions as to how Hank might improve his communication with the CFO regarding the budget.

Several weeks later Hank reported back to the group. He began by saying that on the day of his presentation to Mike he had picked out a very conservative suit. He even thought of buying a new shirt that didn't have French cuffs. Hank knocked before entering the CFO's office and immediately sat down in a chair. He had a pencil in his hand and a folder with him. He told the group how the CFO had noticed the folder and seemed very interested in it.

"This is characteristic of the analytic personality type," Janet said. "I don't take anyone seriously who comes into my office empty-handed. If the person doesn't have a pencil and a notebook, I feel that they aren't serious and won't remember what I say. So I just stop talking."

"Right!" Hank said. "That's just how it was!"

Hank went on to tell Mike that he was sorry the two of them hadn't gotten to know one another better. He told him, "I've got some tickets here for the UNLV basketball game. I was wondering if you'd like to go with me? Do ya' think your wife would let you go for a Saturday afternoon?"

The CFO's eyes had lit up. "I'd really like that."

Hank resisted the impulse to say, "I'll pick you up in a limo and we'll have a high time of it." He suggested they meet at the stadium after lunch instead. Hank then began to present a budget in a more organized way. His wife had helped with the budget during the previous week! He said he had begun to notice that his wife and the CFO had many personality characteristics in common. The group speculated that Hank had married a woman who paid more attention to detail, was a loyal supporter, and was more comfortable as a team member than a quarterback. He agreed that his wife had given him valuable insights into the personality of the CFO.

Personality Partnership

As a result of Janet's insights and the group's help, Hank and the CFO had the beginnings of a new relationship, one based on *personality partnership*. They had become partners by complementing one another's workstyle personality. Each was now able to stop being defensive and move forward in a partnership. Hank now gave more acknowledgment to the CFO for his important role in Hank's success. The CFO felt validated. In his eyes Hank had become more responsible and more serious. As a result he began to be less frugal, less demanding, and less critical of Hank's requests for money.

What has happened here? Nothing changed until there was a greater understanding of personality, of the individual's style and preferences. Hank began to understand the CFO's personality and tried to meet Mike's needs instead of insisting on his own while displaying an overpowering personality style. Mike responded in kind.

But isn't this manipulative? Wasn't Hank taking advantage of this conscientious, analytical type? Wasn't Hank using him and even making fun of him? Well, let's look at it another way. Let's view Hank as treating Mike in a way that the CFO desired to be treated. The CFO was misinterpreting Hank's overtures and expected the tickets and the gestures to be followed by more personal offers of friendship. As Hank began to appreciate the differences in their personalities, they in fact became more friendly and thus better partners. Hank noticed that those things that he loved about his wife, he disliked in the CFO. But he could understand that the love and intimacy that characterized his marriage could also serve as an example for overcoming problems in the workplace. He understood that getting closer to coworkers creates greater respect for their hidden attributes, their "secret" talents, the very positive nature of *every* personality.

Now, let's take a next step. How can you better work with and for those people who have workstyle personalities different from your own? Understanding personality can be one of the most valuable tools for success in the workplace. Take time to review your personal, preferred style and that of significant others in your life and work. You may find that the different styles will make more sense to you if you attempt to fit family members and coworkers into the categories listed in the chart opposite. Work with people who are close to you to test changes. Try new approaches to your usual way of relating.

INCREASING YOUR PEP
PERSONAL EFFECTIVENESS WITH PERSONALITY

This chart provides tips for how you can improve communication with each personality type. When making requests, asking for help, or just improving everyday communication you may find these suggestions helpful. Make *your* changes, and watch *them* change!

For the **Dominator**

Be clear, specific, brief, and to the point.

Stick to business. Come prepared.

Present the facts logically; plan your presentation *efficiently*.

Provide alternatives and choices for the Dominator to consider when making a decision.

Provide facts and figures about probability of success or effectiveness of options.

Motivate and persuade by referring to how this fits in with his or her objectives.

For the **Cooperator**

Start (briefly) with personal chitchat. Break the ice.

Show sincere interest in the Cooperator as a person; comment on pictures on the desk.

Be patient, listen, and be responsive.

Present your case softly, nonthreateningly. Ask *how* questions to draw out the person's opinions.

If you disagree, look for hurt feelings, personal reasons. Try to reassure.

Define clearly (preferably in writing) individual contribution.

For the **Entertainer**

Plan an interaction that supports the Entertainer's dreams and intuitions. Use time to be stimulating. Allow for story telling and entertainment.

Don't deal with details verbally; put them in writing; pin them to modes of action and deadlines.

Provide ideas for implementing action and assign responsibility for follow-up.

Offer special, immediate, and extra incentives for the person's willingness to take risks.

For the **Precisionist**

Prepare your "case" in advance, in writing. Be accurate.

Approach the Precisionist in a straightforward, direct way; stick to business, no chitchat.

Build your credibility by listing pros and cons to any suggestion you make. Provide evidence.

Present specifics and do what you say you can do. Take your time, but be persistent.

Draw up a scheduled approach to implementing action with a step-by-step timetable; assure that there won't be surprises.

Give time to verify reliability of your actions; be accurate, realistic.

Understanding others is the key to meaningful relationships. But relationships, whether on the job or off, can be very hard and require effort. Accept that each person is doing her or his best to survive and get on with the job. Sometimes our attempts to cope are successful. But at other times we simply slip or fail. We can be knocked over by life's pressures. No one is immune to being overwhelmed, stressed out, and emotionally exhausted. But personality education and the resultant personality partnering can be valuable resources for dealing with those "hard knocks" of life and work. Enhance your ability to effectively cope and build stronger relationships by using your personality assets, compensating for areas of difference, building on knowledge, and moving to action.

Recognize

1. You have evaluated your personality style. Did the instruments in this chapter assess you accurately? Is your personality workstyle an effective one for the job you have?
2. Notice how your personality strengths and weaknesses affect your interactions with others in the workplace. Do your workplace and your job mesh with your workstyle personality?
3. Can you identify the personality type with which you work most effectively? Is that the style your boss and close coworkers have? If not, list some effects this has on you and your productivity. Reading this list you may see how some small changes can make a large difference.

Respond

1. Practice approaches to test personality style. For example, approach the desk of a Cooperator and comment on the personal pictures on display. See how your overture is received. Does this interaction produce a positive result? Do you see a difference from previous interactions? This

may suggest a new way to initiate communication with this individual.

2. List elements of your workstyle that you would like to change. For example, if you are an Entertainer, would you like to be more organized? Would you like to pay more attention to detail? Set aside some time to devote to paperwork during the day. Make specific efforts to change.

3. Practice new greetings and approaches to individuals whose personality styles are often different from yours. You may want to rehearse with someone who has a similar style.

Reinforce

Practice these statements:

1. I now discover how wonderful I am. I accept myself and others just as we are.

2. I am open to new ideas. I release the old and welcome the new into my life and job.

3. It is easy for me to reprogram the computer of my mind. I accept new information about others.

4. I see with new eyes. I see others as they wish to be seen. I treat others as they wish to be treated.

To expand and reinforce your knowledge:

1. Look for short courses on personality through extension programs and adult education offerings. Make a commitment to learn more about yourself.

2. Explore personality testing through your company sponsored employee assistance program or the outpatient mental health benefit of your health-care plan.

3. Practice the "golden (personality) rule," Do unto others as you want them to do unto you.

FIVE

Judas, Scape, and Other Goats: Battle Tactics

No reader needs this book to document the day-to-day frustrations that accompany earning a living in America. We all know about that firsthand. Each of us reacts to those frustrations and conflicts. Sadly, many people do so by trying to get even using sabotage, revenge, and even violence. Such behaviors rob us of money and good health, waste time, and disrupt productivity in the work-place.

Retaliation encourages the situation of "me versus them." It is the first step in the process of blaming others, of neglecting the resources you have to solve problems and change conditions. People who sabotage their companies are not necessarily bad employees, vandals, or drug addicts. They are usually ordinary people who have been yelled at once too often when the boss was in a bad mood or when the higher-ups were unreasonable and demanding. They may be people who learned they were expendable after a lifetime of service; perhaps they are the first to have their salaries cut in a budget crunch. They are frequently ordinary people doing ordinary jobs, but who, like you and me, are indeed extraordinary. They see themselves as put upon, sin-gled out, and targeted by others. They are people who have become disillusioned and unproductive for themselves and for others in the workplace. This kind of personal sabotage extracts a high cost, both from the workplace and from the employee.

In his book, *Sabotage in the American Workplace*, Martin Spras defined sabotage as "anything that you do at work that you are not supposed to do." Employees who commit sabotage are not necessarily chronic malcontents, who constantly question company policy, rules, and procedures. Nor are they malingerers. They are frequently smiling, compliant, loyal employees, who quietly go about their jobs and rarely reveal the extent of their desire for revenge, the suppression of their anger, or the activities by which they sabotage both themselves and the company. Keith is an example of such a saboteur.

Keith describes his boss Sasha as a sexist bitch. He talks a lot about reverse discrimination and says that, as a woman, she is power-hungry and trying to get rid of him so she can replace him with a woman. "I can't say I hate the job," Keith says. "I like the people I work with. If I just had a different boss I could be really happy here."

Keith is a supply clerk. The job site is a large supply room, caged for security. One of his jobs is taking inventory, which he dislikes and does poorly. The accuracy of his counts has become a bone of contention between himself and his supervisor. Sasha spot-checks his work, finds errors, and brings them to his attention. She accuses him of sloppiness, lack of attention, and inability to concentrate. She has given Keith an oral warning consistent with the company's personnel guidelines in order for him to correct these deficiencies.

Keith, in retaliation, began to steal from the inventory. Using a complicated system he created in the computer, Keith made it almost impossible for anyone to follow his moves. He later admitted that the items he took were not of much use to him, and most of them ended up in his garage. Keith also sabotaged equipment such as jamming new staplers and returning them to the box, scratching computer disks, or emptying contents of new bottles and replacing the tops. Such petty sabotage created an unknown and unseen havoc as well as a high price in the workplace. What if Keith had simply used a constructive technique to address his grievances? What did he have to lose? Let's look at some alternatives for Keith.

Suppose Keith had confronted his boss not with facts but simply with his views—that is, a *constructive confrontation*. "I feel that you would rather have a woman working in this position. I feel discounted and always picked on." What did Keith have to lose? He had already received an oral warning. He was very unhappy in his job, and he was anxious to leave the company.

Constructive confrontation is a positive way of bringing what bothers us to the attention of others. Too often confrontation is thought of as a fight or an argument, something negative and aggressive. In Keith's case, this confrontation could simply have been statements of feelings. His boss might have responded with ridicule and demeaning statements. Then Keith could have walked away. But the boss might have listened and tried to find better ways of working with Keith. Having been alerted to his feelings, she might have been more sensitive. In any event Keith would probably have felt better had he expressed his feelings and confronted his boss with what he perceived to be her unfair treatment of him.

In yet another scenario, perhaps his boss might have appreciated understanding more about what Keith perceived as her prejudice. Sasha might have been able to reassure him of the fact that she didn't want to replace him in the job, that she valued certain aspects of his performance, but that she wanted some changes. Perhaps the two of them could have worked together to be more constructive and less confrontational. In this story, Keith was laying all the blame on his boss and taking no responsibility. She had "sinned" in his eyes, and he could not forgive her. The process of empowerment, of constructive confrontation, of understanding and assisting others to be our partners begins when we forgive their behavior and get on with the job.

Perhaps in yet another scenario he could have surrendered. Surrender is one of the simplest, and yet most complex, of all the many tools used to change behavior. It's both the safest and riskiest way, the easiest and most difficult step. For many of us, it is the most fear-producing and yet can be the most comforting. Surrender is a straightforward idea, yet it can be one of the hardest to understand. Often the word is ill defined. "How can surrender be good?" you ask. "Isn't it weak to surrender? Haven't I been surrendering all these years to bosses and authority? See where that's gotten me! If I did go along with this surrender idea how is it done? What do I give up, and who do I give it to?"

Often our old definitions of surrender paint a negative picture of weakness and defeat. When people surrender, we might think, they give up themselves or things they want to someone with more power. Perhaps we think of television shows or western movies where the bad guys keep surrendering to the good guys. Maybe it's invading armies we see and the tattered white flag raised over a fort's broken walls. We associate surrender with loss of control over our lives, with failure. But good guys never fail. They never surrender. That's just not the way the world is. Or is it?

Giving Up, Not In

Let's look at a dictionary definition of surrender, one that is frequently overlooked: ". . . to yield to the possession or power of another." Doesn't that really mean *exchange*. Look at common uses of surrender as an exchange: We surrender the title of our old car when we trade it in for a new one. The bank surrenders the promissory note we've signed when we pay off the debt. A defeated army surrenders in exchange for promises of protection and territory. *Thinking of surrender as an exchange, not a defeat, may help us accept the concept more readily.* It can also show us how to surrender. Surrender means exchanging the bad—our old ideas, our old point of view, our old rigidity—for a path that yields more rewards.

What if Keith had simply *surrendered*, using this definition, by exchanging his idea that his boss was wrong for one that accepted her way. "Well," he might say, "She's going to fire me anyway, but I'll try it her way for a while." He could have begun to work more methodically, more carefully. He could have invited her spot-checks, trying to see his work as she saw it. He might have discussed with her specific remarks and behaviors that led him to view her as sexist.

In surrendering, we accept new ideas. Part of this exchange involves learning to trust ourselves and others. To do this, we first may need to sever ties with our old friends—self-will and ego. Admitting our ways are not working, we can try with honesty to open our minds and hearts and see the sources of our fear and anger. Now we are searching for and accepting new ways of behavior. By letting go of fear, anger, and resentment, we can gain freedom, joy, and a sense of control. "I may not like this, but *I've* decided to do it."

YOU'VE GIVEN EVERYTHING, EXCEPT UP

A good way to practice letting go of our fears and our need to control is simply to "fake it." And maybe you'll "make it." Perhaps Keith could have learned better work habits by surrendering his resentment and trying it Sasha's way. "But aren't you asking me to make myself a doormat for these demanding bosses and corporate machines?" No! *Submission* is a counterfeit of surrender. We submit when, in our insecurity, we look for care from someone strong and protective. We submit to another's ideas and opinions, becoming sheep rather than shepherds. This is much easier than taking a deep, honest look at our lives and needed changes. *My new boss is very disciplined and set in her ways. I don't think I could share my views and frustrations with her. She just wouldn't understand.* Or even, *I did everything I could do for him. I practically did his speech for him, and now he's asking for more without even a thank you.*

Only when we've done the groundwork and been willing to let go completely of our old resentments can we change. But how can we translate such a vague concept into something that has real meaning in our lives? There *are* steps that we can take, which may take the mystery out of surrender.

EASY DOES IT, BUT DO IT!

Here is a list of tools, ideas, and actions that can help us understand surrendering. Remember the goal is to create a better work situation *for you!*

Make a List

Take a piece of paper and make a list of what it is you feel or have been told you should change, or you feel are unreasonable demands. Keith might list:

Surrender	In Exchange For
My insistence on my style	More peace each day
My work habits	Less criticism from her
My stealing supplies	Feeling better about myself
My growing resentments	Pride at speaking my mind

The idea is to think in terms of not only giving but receiving. This may be hard to do at first as you fear that if you give up something, or ask for change, you will somehow become vulnerable. If you're not sure what to write, ask a coworker or friend for help.

Don't Go It Alone

There's a tool that is very effective in the fight against anger, fear, and resentment—speech. Sometimes the hardest things to surrender are our insecurity and pride. We still think it's weak to ask for help, as if we're waging the "me-against-the-world" war. Be honest. How many battles have we won with our "me, myself, and I" army? Probably few, if any. We all need help sometimes. We need someone to listen. We need another's perspective on the things we find troubling. And who better to listen, understand, and help us than someone who's just like us? Take a deep breath and ask for a coworker's perspective. Be willing to communicate. Be willing to accept the help others are waiting to offer.

Act As If

Sometimes we may identify something we know we need to surrender, but we can't seem to make the break. It's "too important," or perhaps it's something we think only we can solve. *No one else really knows what I do. No one else sees that side of the boss.* Well, we can continue to carry these millstones around our neck or we can "act as if." Act as if we no longer needed to be right when we come into conflict with our boss. Act as if we aren't angry when our boss schedules us to work on Saturday. Act as if we no longer feel guilty when we find a lost file that we had accused *him* of losing.

A look at Doreen's story will show us how to "act as if." She had been unwilling to surrender her pride. Doreen, an administrative associate, worked for Tim, who was a poor communicator. She made up for this by "mind reading." She tried to anticipate the needs of both the department and Tim. Her performance evaluations reflected his appreciation for her good work. However, her raises did not. Then she was passed over for consideration for a newly created position as market analyst with a commensurate pay increase. She spoke to the human resources director asking for reasons. "Yes," replied Paulette the HR director, "You meet the qualifications, but Tim feels you aren't a real team player. He praises your initiative but feels you wouldn't do well working with the team that requires input to the analyst's concerns and a synthesizing of their ideas."

Doreen was shocked and very angry. She decided to confront Tim. She was surprised at how attentively Tim, who sat quietly and met her gaze very directly, listened to her. When he began to speak, she had yet another shock. She realized her attempts to "mind read" had really been a rationalization for her own self-will and desire to do the job "her way." She saw that when Tim did attempt to direct her efforts, she had pooh-poohed his ideas and discounted his comments. She disliked what she was hearing and knew she would have to change.

"So I resolved to really listen, to be patient," she said. "Tim's way of speaking is very slow, and I was jumping in too soon. I was frustrated. At first it was hard for me. But you should see me now! I'm really a team listener!"

Doreen "acted as if." She showed her resolve to change and learn from others. Soon the acting (that she felt like listening to people) became the real thing. Feeling "a part of" began to feel natural.

Assess Your Teachability

Teachability can be described as our ability to learn. Some people are more teachable than others. Some of us think we know all the answers. We may be rigid, inflexible, and limited by the boundaries of our fears. We aren't very teachable. Teachability, however, can be learned. How teachable are you? When you're wrong, do you refuse to admit it? Do you frequently argue with others? When you're involved in problems that aren't your fault, do you seek to explain your role? Do you replay the scenes in which you were wronged over and over in your mind?

Your answers may reveal how your antagonistic character can impede growth. To become teachable, you must admit you don't know everything. Then you become vulnerable—a condition many people find uncomfortable. The opposite of antagonistic—highly agreeable on the outside and secretly seething—also impedes growth and change. But the rewards of teachability are great. We begin to learn how to exchange anger and rigidity, silence and resentment, for serenity and flexibility. We begin to grow more creative, more comfortable, and more secure in our new lifestyle. More in control and powerful!

Be King or Queen for a Day

We can indulge ourselves occasionally, but in a different way. Instead of fantasizing about grandiose schemes and perfectionistic plans to get even or plot a *Nine to Five*-style revenge, we can treat ourselves like kings or queens in different ways. We can take time to enjoy a walk at lunch, a movie after work, or a *real*

break in the morning and afternoon. It's healthy to try to escape
what's uncomfortable. Change is often uncomfortable. A bit of
fresh air and a change of scene can help us return to responsibilities with renewed energy.

Give In Occasionally

If we find ourselves often quarreling with people and feeling
defiant, remember that's how frustrated children behave. We
should stand our ground on what we know is right but do so
calmly. And we should be ready to admit that we *could be* wrong.
It's easier on our systems to give in occasionally. If we yield, we'll
frequently find that others will too. The result may be gaining
relief from tension and feeling that we've achieved a practical
solution. We'll have exchanged immature behavior for relief from
stress. We're practicing to surrender.

Take One Thing at a Time

Given to thinking in grandiose terms, we are ready to surrender *everything*. We'll quit smoking, lose weight, begin exercising, find a relationship, return to school, and get a better
job. But this isn't surrender. To attempt to give up all your bad
habits at once is setting yourself up for failure. Maybe you're
trying to do too much at once. Beat your bad habits one step
at a time.

Do Something for Others

Distracting yourself is important for a successful surrender,
and it's also a good practice for life in general. Spend time helping someone. Volunteer in a community center or local school.
Think of this as a surrender and exchange. Don't be embarrassed
to say, "I'm doing this for selfish reasons. By helping others, I can
learn how to surrender my will, desire, and impulses." Sound
strange? Just try it.

Slow Down the Pace

The world is not a race. Practice driving within the speed limit and letting cars pass you on the freeway. Don't aggressively compete in your exercise program. When you're tempted to make a quick response, take a deep breath and let the other person complete his or her thought. Instead of watching the television, listen to soothing music. Take a leisurely bath instead of a quick shower. Exchange the frantic pace of "hi, good-bye" conversations for higher quality time with other people. Relax your sense of perfectionism. Don't scrub the bathtub with a toothbrush!

Consult an Expert

Our attempts to change old habits and attitudes may produce conflict and stress. The interacting forces both inside and around us tend to have a cumulative effect on our mental health, making little things seem worse. It may be useful to seek the help of a counseling or guidance service, a therapist, or other mental health professional. Ask a coworker or friend for a recommendation. Most companies today have employee assistance programs (EAPs) providing prepaid counseling for employees and family members. Ask your human resource or personnel director if your company offers this benefit.

Write

Putting pen to paper forces us to stop and think. We sort out words, feelings, and impressions. We may be able to understand an otherwise hopelessly confusing situation only after we've taken the time to put our impressions of it on paper. When we read it we may notice things we hadn't seen before. We're able to think much more clearly and in the right perspective. Self-honesty is the cornerstone of this writing. We can fill hundreds of notebooks with meanderings on our daily life and get no closer to the peace and serenity we crave if we lack honesty. Only when we're honest about our feelings can we begin to identify those things that make us anxious, resentful, or angry. This exercise can help us see areas of our lives we're reluctant to release.

Join the Comedy Club

Changing, coping, and the normal course of any workday produce stress. But a healthy dose of laughter helps. A sense of humor shows us that being in control is not always vital. Can you laugh at yourself? Quit trying so hard to figure out what *surrender* is and how to do it. This, coupled with a few belly laughs, is surrender at its best.

Recognize the Levels of Power

To most of us power has a limited definition: the ability to do anything we want. That immature view of power feeds an inflated ego. But there's a higher form of power. It's achieved by recognizing needs beyond our own. Meeting other people's needs moves us a step higher on the power scale. Again, exchange produces a form of power that we can tap. By accepting another's perspective we don't lose our ability to exercise power. We give up the self-centered preoccupation with our needs only to discover that many of our needs can be met by reaching out to others.

Try a Spiritual Program

Most religious and spiritual systems make use of surrender. Some of us have long since given up on the concept of formal religion, but we may retain abiding faith in the ways of nature or the power of logic. Still others recognize the power of a twelve-step program and the fellowship of the group, choosing the group as a Higher Power. We need to be tolerant and accepting of spiritual principles. The point is to find something that works for us. We can talk and write, but there comes a time when action must be taken. Spiritual support in any form can be an effective tool for coping with stress.

Joel describes his experience. When caught in a merger-buyout, his position as a field representative for a medical services company changed literally overnight. "I know I had to 'give in,'" he said. "I had lost my faith in this corporation and the workplace in general. I realized I had made my work my religion. Then I sat down with a friend, and he asked me to try to think of something in whose power and constancy I could truly believe. He said not to worry about whether that something could remove all my anxieties and shortcomings, just to think of something I could believe would always be there.

"Well, I'm a surfer, so the first thing that popped into my mind was the beautiful ocean. I always felt closer to the true nature of things when I was in the water, like I was a real part of the cycle. That was the closest thing I knew of then to a spiritual experience. My friend suggested that the next time I went in the water to let it flow over me and carry away those unwanted anxieties and fears. He said it sounded like I'd already been doing it without knowing. But, to me, the conscious awareness made the difference. I always left the beach freer and more joyous than before."

Joel found, after searching and experimentation, a support that he could relate to spiritually and emotionally. A belief system may help us discover faith within ourselves as we surrender those things that keep our lives frustrating and stressful. One way to increase our conscious contact with spiritual support is through prayer and meditation. These are invaluable tools in the surrender process.

Use a "Boss Box"

Try making a Boss Box. Joel tried this, too. "I found a little tin box I had saved from childhood and put in it a list of things that were bugging me. The act of writing down those things was powerful in itself, but actually putting them in my tin box and closing the lid was the most freeing thing I'd ever done. I knew then that they were out of my hands. I found that with my Boss

Box I had more patience to wait and just do my job. I use my little Boss Box quite often still and sometimes, to my surprise, I even forget what I've put in there. I know that the sooner I'm willing to surrender my concerns, then they will be lifted from me that much more quickly. I no longer have to share my life with my obsessions."

Surrender, we find, is no longer the demon of failure we once thought it to be. It ceases to be a struggle between the good guys and the bad guys. All we need to do is admit our shortcomings, be open-minded about alternatives to our own behavior and perspective, and then be willing to surrender old ideas to gain greater rewards.

> **"Do not seek so much to be consoled, as to *console;* do not seek so much to be understood, as to *understand;* do not seek so much to be loved, as to *love."*
>
> ST. FRANCIS OF ASSISI

Recognize

1. Recognize examples of blaming, sabotage, and struggle in your job.
2. When evaluating injustices and grievances, ask yourself, *Have I ever done something like this?* Try and remember a specific incident. Now ask yourself, *Did someone help me or overlook my mistake?* If the answer is yes, perhaps you can pass *that* along, rather than anger and resentment.

Respond

1. Respond by listing some exchanges for each situation.
2. Read the want ads. This may give you a better perspective on making the job you have more satisfying.

Reinforce

1. Before you say anything to anyone, ask yourself three things: 1) *Is it true?* 2) *Is it kind?* 3) *Is it necessary?* Use this for self talk. It will eliminate such self-defeating statements as, "I'm stupid."

2. Practice these statements:
   - I choose balance. My life is complete with more than work.
   - I have the right to say no. I choose for myself.
   - I have a history of success. I have many talents and skills. I am not my job.

SIX

The Company Family:
The Ties That Strangle

"Memory can be a great substitute for thinking."

> BERNARD G. RETHOVE, President and CEO
> Microdot Industries

"We need to believe in ourselves but not to believe that life is easy."

> JOHN GARDNER, Author
> *Self-Renewal*

Most of us learn our "people" and communication skills in the family. All too often family communication is characterized by eccentricity and, sometimes, dysfunction. Because the workplace is structured a lot like a family, individuals often fall into roles created for them in our childhood. In other words, at work we act like children. When an employee experiences discomfort and dissatisfaction with a job, he or she often focuses in a myopic and self-centered way on his or her own unhappiness without looking to the larger picture of the group or family process and dynamics.

What has a family to do with a corporate structure? Any group of people is likely to take on the structure of a family. All too often, in the workplace, groups of people model dysfunctional families. That is, people who make up the group, the team, or the corporation act and react in ways learned in the families in which they were born and grew up, the family of origin. If that family was healthy, the child had a chance to learn from appropriate models of communication and interaction. If the family was dysfunctional, the child, now adult, will face many more challenges than the adult who learned from a more functional model.

Ann Wilson Schaef, in *The Addictive Organization*, describes the ever-increasing dysfunction of the corporate world. "We have begun to realize that many of the behaviors considered 'normal' for individuals in organizations are actually a repertoire of an active addict or a recovering codependent."

A dysfunctional family functions by controlling individual freedom. A dysfunctional system operates in the same manner, presenting limited options for employee roles or behaviors, and even limiting the way a person should think. In each dysfunctional family, it is important that certain roles are played or the system will be disrupted. The same is true in a corporation. It is important that those around you keep you in your role in order to keep the whole system in balance. Or out of balance, as the case may be.

THE AUDITION

What are those roles? Well, in a corporation, the boss, whether the head of the team, the head of the department, or the head of the corporation, is viewed as the Daddy. Because of the continued male dominance in America's corporate structure, the father figure heads the hierarchy of the dysfunctional "family." An employee's experience in his or her own family of origin, a loving father or an abusive one, a tyrant or a benevolent dictator, sets a model for this interaction. When the boss is viewed as the father of the family, this leaves narrowly defined and limited roles for the rest of the "family," that is, the other employees.

The next most influential role in the group or family is that of the Mom. This person is responsible for caretaking, placating, or perhaps even passively dominating. In many families the mother is in fact the head of the system. Once the partner-dictatorship is established, whether abusive or benevolent, father and mother (sometimes both are roles played by one person) set the tone for the family. Perhaps the Mom is played by a management team, senior VP, or team leader. The role is to placate or mediate between disruptive forces. The Mom often says to employees, "Don't let the boss find out about that. Let's keep this between us. If you do that the CEO will be unhappy." In the dysfunctional system the placator alternately uses the image of the father figure to stress, punish, and reward the employee.

The employees are left with limited and stereotypic roles: the Hero, the Mascot, the Scapegoat, and the Lost Child. All are subservient or auxiliary. Let's examine each of these roles and see how they fit in the corporate structure. As you read, you may find it helpful to make notes on the relevance of the roles to your organization, personalizing each role.

The Hero

The Hero is usually the oldest child in the family, who early on assumes burdens that are inappropriate to the child's age and to what should be expected of an older sibling. With the employee in a dysfunctional system, the dynamics are the same. The Hero is the employee who assumes burdens above and beyond the job description. This employee is the "responsible one" and may be a workaholic. He or she is frequently exhausted, always under stress, and is rigid, aggressive, constantly on the go, and often self-righteous. The Hero is frequently quite charming and uses his or her charisma to advantage. Frequently, such behavior masks procrastination, insecurity, neediness, inability to set limits or delegate, and a need for acceptance for "being" rather than "doing." Because the Hero in a family is still a child, he or she competes for the parents' attention and approval. As other children enter the system, the conflict intensifies.

The Hero in the workplace can be a very disruptive influence, often setting a frenetic pace for others, failing to share responsibilities or credit, yet all the while feeling alone. "I'm the only one who can do something right. I do things the way the boss (father/mother) wants it to be done." This is the employee who can make others feel guilty and resentful because of the long hours and effort they appear to give to the job. Finally, this person wants and needs the attention and approval of the authority figure(s). In the workplace this employee needs to be recognized for being more productive than the other employees. This employee always needs *more*. Behind the back of this employee, coworkers may secretly resent, pity, or generally fail to respect him for his workstyle and work ethic. This workaholic employee is never finished and never feels satisfied. This role can have a devastating effect on anyone who assumes it.

"I felt as if I had to do everything myself because, after all, I couldn't trust others to do anything as well as I could. If you want something done right, do it yourself." Elena is a thirty-six-year-old owner and operator of a small but lucrative insurance brokerage. Although she had been plagued by constant headaches, back problems, and had been warned by her physician to slow down and relax more, Elena felt that she couldn't. When she took time off from work, her employees made costly mistakes. Elena complained that her sales people made unrealistic promises to clients, promises that could have had heavy legal ramifications, and errors on contracts that would be costly to the company. In her absence she complained that her employees also ran up expensive phone bills and misplaced important messages. Elena's feelings of frustration and helplessness were real. "After all the training sessions I've done with them, why did they keep making the same mistakes over and over again? I thought having a staff would ease my workload, but I spent most of my time cleaning up their messes!" Elena vacillated between treating her people with hostility and patience. In one meeting she would rant and rave about their incompetence, and in the next she would give them a pat on the back and a pep talk about how good things were going to be.

Elena had set up unrealistic expectations for herself and then had projected them onto her staff. As long as we make such unrealistic demands of ourselves, we will continue to fall short. And if we don't live up to our own expectations, we will keep blaming other people. Elena was obviously demanding perfection from her employees, a perfection that she sought for herself at a tremendous price to herself and, ultimately, to her own business.

Elena felt trapped. Just two months earlier she had signed a five-year lease for her new, expanded office. What had seemed like a good idea and a wonderful dream was quickly turning into a nightmare. Although she was not aware of them, Elena had options. In any problem situation our emotional investment distorts our vision. Perhaps you can see options for Elena. She could turn over the management of her company to someone else, hire an office manager, fire her salespeople and hire more competent ones, retrain her existing staff, or sell her business. The list could go on. Until Elena looked at her motives and expectations of herself, she wouldn't be able to see how she had set herself up to fail. *Owning a business and managing a staff feed my ego, but is it worth my physical and mental well-being? Should my business take priority over my family? Do I really want the responsibility anymore?* Once she had taken the time to ask these questions, and answer them, decisions, and thus action steps, became more clear.

Elena called a meeting with her staff and announced, "I've come to a decision. I find a large organization too taxing on my health, so I've decided to work on my own." Not long after reorganizing, another insurance broker walked into her quiet office. His first thought was that the bottom had dropped out of her business. He asked, "Where's everybody? Did they all walk out on you? Are you going out of business?"

"No," Elena replied, "I let them all go. My business is better than ever." What looked like a failure from outward appearances was really a true success story.

The initial change began when Elena stopped feeling she had no control over her circumstances. The biggest change occurred when she stopped blaming others and began to examine her own priorities. Both took less then twenty minutes. Soon, Elena's physical problems subsided. She now has more time and energy for her family, and her business runs profitably and with less effort.

Let Me Entertain You!

Another role that is usually played in groups is that of the Mascot (or Clown or Rebel-Without-a-Clue, take your pick). This employee entertains and distracts the dysfunctional family from conflict. When stress gets too high, the Mascot is there to relieve the pressure. This person "tap dances," cracks jokes, and misbehaves in order to get the attention of the authority figure(s) and take the focus off of the real problems.

In a dysfunctional family the father may be drunk and the mother may threaten to leave. This Mascot child then gets into trouble at school, creating a drama, and leading the focus away from the mother's threats and the father's alcoholism. In an organization, it is very much the same. When the stakes are high—it looks like a merger might be pending and layoffs coming—this employee distracts other employees from constructive activity by refusing to take things seriously, by suggesting misbehavior, or by creating rumors that feed distraction rather than problem-solving or fact-finding.

Very often the Mascot is well liked, popular, and witty. The person may be viewed as eccentric. "That's just the way Ted is. You know Ted, he's always making a joke!" This can be the "bad boy" (or girl) in a company. He or she is the rebel, or disrupter, who is benevolently viewed by other employees, given a pat on the head, and perhaps not taken seriously. This employee is probably unhappy and not very productive. Such an employee's sense of self-esteem is negatively affected by this kind of behavior.

The Scapegoat

The Scapegoat can be a person or group of people on whom we blame a problem. "Well, if personnel would just get its act

together . . ." "If marketing weren't so demanding . . ." "If corporate didn't make such arbitrary decisions . . ." The Scapegoat
allows us to give up our responsibility for solving the problems.
We now have an excuse for not trying to change situations. We
blame and hope that the problems will go away. In the family,
this is the child who gets sick when the parents are drinking too
much. This is the child who often "gets caught" when siblings
quarrel and misbehave, or becomes the suspected culprit when
mischief is discovered. All fingers automatically point to the
Scapegoat.

The Scapegoat is a role that many people are taught to play
and continue to play as adults. This person may resemble the
Mascot—entertaining and rebellious, but always taking the focus
off of us and the real problems. The dynamics of blaming are
necessary for dysfunctional systems to maintain homeostasis—the
status quo.

"I worked for a large telemarketing firm," relates Salina, who
experienced firsthand the enmeshment of these roles. "We actually referred to our supervisor as 'Big Daddy' even though she
was a woman. I don't know where the name 'Big Daddy' came
from. I just know all the employees called her that." She was
erratic in her praise as well as her criticism of us. We could always
count on her to say something, but we never knew if it would
be good or bad. Sometimes I would reach very high totals of
sales and closings. Yet she would criticize me for not doing more.
On other days when I looked a little blue or came in a couple
of minutes late, she might be very sympathetic. I know that she
made me feel like a child. That was bad enough, but the
employee who got all of our sympathy was Joanna. She couldn't
do anything right and got nothing but blame. I wondered why she
stayed. I would see her accused of the most outrageous things. I
think her mistreatment of Joanna hurt me more than her mistreatment of me."

Salina describes very graphically the process of dysfunction in
the workplace. A competent woman, a good worker, she fell into
the pattern of childlike discomfort, even fear, around "Big Daddy,"

the person who was unpredictable in both praise and discipline. Like a child, Salina began to second-guess and "read minds," trying very hard to please and forgetting work goals. She eventually left the company. "I needed to be in a situation where I was rewarded more consistently. 1 was making good money in that company and my commissions were high. But the stress of trying to anticipate the moods of my supervisor and the unpredictability of the system just took too much of a toll. And I just couldn't stand seeing anyone abused like Joanna was."

Where, Oh Where . . .

Another role played in the family is that of the Lost Child. This is a "good" child who does what is expected, does not create problems, but all too often is overlooked when rewards and attention are doled out. This employee is a team player, but doesn't have the flair, the drama, or the problems to draw the attention of "the boss." This employee may feel overlooked and unappreciated. This worker frequently picks up the pieces for other employees then feels resentful because no credit or attention is paid to his or her efforts on behalf of the team.

The lost child, or the lost employee, is a valuable employee, yet one who is prey to other job offers or quietly seeks a new position. If you are such a person, you do not have to change your job; rather, change your behavior in order to get the attention you deserve, to receive the appreciation you feel you've earned. If this is a coworker, you may be helpful in assisting that person to become more vocal in order for the team to function more productively. This person would make an excellent partner.

HAPPILY EVER AFTER

In this chapter we see that groups of people in companies, as in the society and in families, tend to be more alike than they are different. They accept or take on roles that may not be comfortable, but are at least familiar. Sometimes the behavior of one person dictates to the other members of the group the roles available to them. When the employee becomes the Daddy, the Mom, or the Mascot, the other employees escape roles that require confrontation or effort. A person who might do well as a supervisor may back down or take a more subservient role rather than compete with a Hero, who has already assumed that personality.

The corporation is not a family. These roles need not be real. Reality is job descriptions and behaviors needed to do the jobs. Your next step is to separate dysfunctional and remembered roles from actual job descriptions, personalities, and necessary functions in the workplace. In looking at these dysfunctional roles we see that there are specific dynamics that allow the roles to continue to be played.

These roles and the dynamics that keep them in place are not easy to understand. If this is your first introduction to the concepts, you may wish to do some additional reading or participate in self-help groups and twelve-step programs like Codependent Anonymous (CODA) and Adult Children of Alcoholics (ACA). These are listed in the white pages of many phone books and in the yellow pages under "Alcohol." If not, simply call Alcoholics Anonymous for a referral number. Another good source for low-cost information on these subjects is Hazelden, the largest international publisher of recovery pamphlets, books, tapes, etc. Call 800-328-9000 for a free copy of their mail-order catalogue. If you're ready to move on, the first step in dealing with codependency in a company is to identify the roles that people on your team, or in your "family," may be playing. Relate those dynamics to your own job. Then, it's time to consider a change or take a risk by changing your own behavior and stepping out of the assigned role.

MIND YOUR OWN MIND!

Enabling is a term describing behavior, conscious and unconscious, that allows or encourages addiction. It is a dynamic that maintains dysfunctional behavior. For example, a husband may wish that his wife stop drinking. When she turns down wine at dinner, which he enjoys in moderation, he may say, "Oh, come on, just have one glass." In this way he falsely pretends that his wife can limit her drinking to one glass of wine, denying her alcoholism and giving her a mixed message. On one hand he wants her to quit drinking, but on the other hand he says it is okay to drink. He stays in control; she is off-balance as he *enables* her to drink.

In an organization, people enable by using silence, by failing to confront, by going along with the group, by acceding to peer pressure. For example, a secretary is asked by his boss if he would mind working late tonight. Instead of saying, "Yes, I would mind, I have already made plans with my family," or, "No, I wouldn't mind just this once, but I will make up the time with a long lunch tomorrow," or clarifying that his additional hours would be recompensed as overtime pay, the secretary responds by saying, "Well . . ."

Then the boss says, "It's up to you."

And the secretary, feeling pressured, says, "It is okay, I guess. . . ."

This is an example of enabling behavior. The secretary enabled the boss to get what he wanted by not speaking up or asking for time to think. Both engaged in dysfunctional behavior, creating resentment and anger on the part of the employee, who failed to be recompensed for the additional work, and who will probably get even.

As My Company Turns

Drama or *soap opera* is another dynamic that maintains dysfunction. Soap opera is unnecessary drama around day-to-day operations. Drama in an organization usually has to do with gossip, distraction, and overreaction.

Janet describes an experience in the data entry department where seventeen men and women worked at entering data from insurance forms. Some might see the work as boring, but it is a critically important function in the organization. Often this group distracts itself with gossip and chitchat. They still maintain a high level of productivity because they are experienced. Janet had just walked in and heard everyone conversing loudly. She asked what the buzz was about.

"Mandatory carpooling!" was the answer. "They are going to make us all carpool. They've got a consultant coming in. They're laying out grids, and we are going to be told who lives in our neighborhood. Then we are going to be given thirty days to start carpooling with those people."

Janet laughed, "Where did such a rumor get started?"

"Well, it is very serious!" they all chimed in.

Janet knew that mandatory carpooling was a ludicrous idea and wouldn't happen. Surely it violated several civil rights and would have been a first for any company! However, the group was so invested in the drama and so distracted from their work they failed to recognize any rational input.

I've Got a Secret

Secrets is another dynamic that maintains the status quo of addiction in the workplace and is necessary for dysfunctional families. Consider the parable of the elephant in the living room. A family is sitting around watching television. Their vision is blocked by a large elephant. A visitor comes to the door, comes in, and sees the elephant in the living room. The visitor wonders why they don't move the elephant. No one mentions the elephant, and the visitor is invited to sit down and watch television with the group. All of them conscientiously ignore the elephant. The elephant of metaphor has many forms—alcoholism, child abuse, and domestic violence are only a few. Is there an elephant in your workplace?

Ramon is a newly elected vice president in a large software-development corporation. Upon promotion to vice president he was given access to a company car. He was happily surprised to discover this was one of the perks of his job. At the same time this company was engaged in severe cost-cutting. Expenses of all sorts were under close scrutiny. Ramon wondered why the company continued to provide a seemingly nonessential benefit. The firm was relatively small and did not attract the types of executives who required such perks. One of Ramon's first high-level corporate meetings involved a budget review of the administrative aspects of the program. Ramon knew that expenses such as travel and corporate cars would be part of this review, and he expected to lose his company car.

Each member of the group, all vice presidents and above, had been provided a copy of the budget for review. Ramon had conscientiously reviewed his and made many notations that he might bring up in the meeting. As the meeting proceeded, Ramon became aware of an undercurrent in the room. He realized that this budget was not going to be seriously attacked. He found himself pulling back when items he had marked for discussion were brought to the table. He waited for the company cars to be considered. The item was passed over by the CFO chairing the meeting. Ramon did not speak up. He left the meeting wondering about the apparent hypocrisy of this group. They were requiring severe cutbacks on supplies and operating expenses for the departments, and yet they were unwilling to recognize some fat in their own budget. At the same time, as a new vice president, he was reluctant to mention this fact to anyone. Doing so would have proved risky, and so his realization became his secret.

A secret is not necessarily something dramatic, exciting, or an item that will tear down the foundations of a corporation with scandal and notoriety. A secret is simply something we observe, are bothered by, and fail to address. Like secrets in families, secrets in organizations are usually very destructive.

You Are Me, Babe

In understanding dysfunctional systems, the term codependence represents an important component. (Codependence may be defined as *a constellation of behaviors that emerge from exposure to addictive systems.*)

The codependent is characterized by a behavioral style in which emotional needs and responses are dictated by the actions and reactions of other people. In other words, the codependent looks to others to make him or her feel good. At the same time a perceived slight or careless word from another can cause feelings of rejection or injury.

The codependent in the workplace is a passive-aggressive communicator specializing in highly indirect communication. This results in mixed messages and confused communication. Often the codependent will agree on the surface, express the passive-aggressive component through some subtle sabotage such as missing deadlines, overly perfectionistic work, demands, etc. Frequently others are blamed for resultant delays and mistakes.

Here are some other traits associated with codependence.

Making nice:	Hides hidden or denied hostility; covers repressed emotions.
Serving others:	Provides a facade of helpfulness often accompanied by a long-suffering attitude; martyrdom; "It's all on my shoulders" statements.
Caretaking:	Often takes the form of a domination and manipulation. A substance-abusing partner is often associated with codependent caretakers.
Good listening:	May disguise a need to control and manipulate others through rumor, manipulation, and indirect communication.
Victimization:	Related to the picture of an overburdened martyr, the codependent often portrays self as a victim, or is central to many "dramas"—usually self-created.
Depression:	Is often associated with codependence as the individual's control and manipulation tactics fail to produce the desired feelings, e.g., love, affection, loyalty.

Negativity:	Being a "wet blanket," opposing change and generally expressing insecurity and rigidity of thinking when creativity or movement is called for in the work-place.

Notice that any one of these traits taken alone may be normal, ordinary, even positive, such as good listening. Codependent people exhibit several of these characteristics in the extreme. Individuals emerging from alcoholic families are likely to exhibit code-pendence to some degree. When the dynamics of the dysfunctional family are recreated in the workplace, it is easy for an adult child of addictive parents to fall into old behaviors. Addiction, whether in the form of workaholism or substance abuse, occurs only with the support of codependence.

CAN WE TALK?

In summary, there are many negative aspects in bringing the model of family into the workplace. We have described the dys-functional family. But can the family model serve as a positive example for dynamics in the workplace? Absolutely! This can be a good way of helping employees to redefine their roles, change dynamics of their behavior, and stop the elements of dysfunction. In a happy, healthy family, communication is direct and open. Confrontation is not feared, and emphasis is placed on changing negative behavior rather than blaming individuals. The same is true of an organization. When dysfunctional behavior and the enabling dynamics are removed, there is freedom for direct com-munication, constructive confrontation, greater creativity and pro-ductivity. Employees then are free to experience different roles, including leadership.

And the roles that we have previously described can be very useful when communication is open. At times a Mascot can dis-tract the group to break the level of tension. Sometimes a group should blame the anonymous corporate entity, the budget, or the economy in order to take the focus off their powerlessness. It is frequently useful to have someone protect us or go to bat for us or support us if we are in a confrontation, like healthy parents and Heros might do.

The problem exists not in the words or roles of mother, father, child, but only when roles are established to limit choices. If we function without choices, or as though we were not responsible, mature adults, then we as employees will not be productive in situations that require creativity, communication, and problem solving. The loyalties of a family, the love and interdependence of the family, can serve as positive examples of how a company can function. These are the qualities of empowerment.

Recognize

1. Identify the role which you play in your organization (note that you may play more than one role).
2. Identify the aspects of this role that are positive and the aspects that are negative.
3. Would you like to change this role?
4. What role, or combination of roles, would you prefer to play in your organization?
5. What hinders you from playing this role? Pay special attention to enabling, secrets, codependency, and drama.

Respond

Having identified the roles and the dynamics keeping this role in place, respond with your feelings about each aspect of these roles and dynamics. For example, "When I recognize that I am *enabling* my boss to give me vague directions, I feel like a kid. I'm angry at myself and embarrassed." Or, "I see that I am most like the Hero. I feel best when I know someone else needs me. I don't like having to do so much work to feel good about myself.

1. Make two columns on a sheet of blank paper, and on one side list the role or dynamic (e.g., secrets, enabling) and in the other column the feelings that that role elicits in you (e.g., anger, fear).

Reinforce

1. Commit to explore the roles in your own family of origin. Perhaps attending a twelve-step self-help group such as Adult Children of Alcoholics or Codependents Anonymous can be a first step.
2. Check local bookstores in the self-help section for books on dysfunctional families and alcoholism.
3. Repeat this statement: "Time has healed the wounds of the past. I am free to be me."

SEVEN

A Seven on the Richter Scale: Coping With Anger

"Peace is not something you wish for. It is something you make, something you do, something you are, and something you give away."

ROBERT FULGHUM

"The only way you can achieve true revenge is not to let your enemies cause you to self-destruct."

HARVEY MACKAY

In any situation of change, conflict, or misunderstanding, there is anger. Anger frequently masks fear. Fear in situations of conflict and change is very predictable. And with anger there is usually blame, for oneself and for others. Anger is one of the most destructive forces in the workplace today. It is ultimately a fatal emotion. Studies show that about 20 percent of us have hostility levels high enough to be dangerous—to our own health and to those around us. Hostility level is associated with increased smoking, drinking, eating, and weight gain. Hostility has long been a well-established contributor to coronary risk and heart disease, as well as myriad other illnesses.

It's likely you have experienced the relationship between anger, depression, resentment, and low self-esteem. You know about the aches and pains that come from tension. The fatigue and lack of joy that ensue as days are increasingly filled with the burden of frustration and suppressed rage.

Paul describes the hostile atmosphere he endured for over three years in his position as quality engineer in a large fabrication department of a microchip company.

"The head of the company had a philosophy that people worked best under stress. The senior managers emulated him by putting impossible deadlines on projects, arbitrarily rejecting products, and trashing work that was already passed for shipment. At first I didn't understand, then one of the team leaders under my supervision clued me in. I became very angry. I tried to talk to my department head about the destructive nature of this practice. I even naively quoted studies showing how reward motivates employees and negativity reduces productivity. Once more I got 'clued in.' 'This is how the president works,' I was told.

"Now I was not only angry, but felt powerless. I was trapped. I had just relocated my wife and two kids—one just starting a new middle school—and my wife had found a job she really loved in the new area. And the benefits were good. Plus I began to feel I needed to protect the fabrication workers. By staying I could absorb some of the craziness and let them keep working. Boy, was I wrong!

"Headaches, nightmares, a rash on both arms, and general irritability were only a few of the symptoms that came with this deal. I went to my doctor about the rash, and we started to talk. The whole story came out. He said I should quit. I just laughed. I found myself avoiding meetings so I wouldn't blurt something out. I missed some important design changes that ultimately impacted the workers I was trying to protect. I took more sick days and just sat at home watching television. I was drinking, and I don't even like the stuff. And I got angrier and angrier."

Paul was lucky. This privately held company was purchased by a larger concern, and then everything changed. With the new management, a different philosophy—one that Paul subscribed to—came into being. He felt "saved." His methods were now valued. But Paul didn't just relax. He decided to get some help for the lingering resentment and anger he felt. Paul saw an ad for an anger management course, and enrolled. *Anger management* can be defined as taking the positive aspects of an emotion (energy, adrenaline, discomfort) and turning them to positive use. At the same time, anger management includes controlling or eliminating the negative aspects (self-denigration, acting out, harming others). Note that this definition does not mean you never get angry. Accepting life on life's terms is a part of any plan for improved communication. The emotion of anger has a positive and protective value to humans.

To begin a program of anger management, let's define a few terms. *Confrontation* is a word that most people react to in a negative manner. "I hate confrontation," is a common response. Or, "I'm uncomfortable with confrontation." "I'm not good at confronting anyone." A slightly different view defines *constructive confrontation* as a technique of bringing feelings and facts to bear on a situation, with a plan in mind for positive resolution. Thus, confrontation takes on a positive and less aggressive tone. Constructive confrontation includes elements of self-assessment, rehearsal, objectivity, and sometimes coaching.

Jackson teaches in a community college and shares a desk with a coworker in a cubbyhole of an office. Jackson comes in on alternate days to his peer, so the arrangement should have worked out. But each time Jackson arrived, he found the desk cluttered with crumpled paper, dirty coffee cups, and food scraps. At first Jackson cleaned the desk, thinking his coworker might get the message. When the trash continued to appear, Jackson left it stacked in a pile with his colleague's name on it. Nothing helped.

Jackson complained to his wife over and over. When she suggested he confront his coworker, he replied, "It's just so petty. I don't want to make an issue of it." Yet, just as Jackson made the statement to his wife, he realized what an issue it had become for him. Recalling a recent training he had attended on negotiation and confrontation, he decided to try for a positive approach and deal directly with his peer.

The technique of constructive confrontation emphasizes the positive elements of direct and honest communication. In this example Jackson had become increasingly preoccupied with the problem and was taking it home; he realized that his indirect ways of dealing with the situation would not work to relieve his discomfort.

Jackson took action. He came to the shared office when he knew his coworker would be available. Simply and directly he stated his request for a cleaner workspace. His deskmate seemed a little embarrassed and agreed to dispose of the trash and clean the desk after he left each day. Jackson thanked him and left. What had become a nagging obsession was dead within the space of minutes, and Jackson felt tremendous relief.

ANGER KILLS

Mario's anger caused emotional pain as he endured a hostile and demeaning situation at work. But he also began to have physical pain. His story begins with his boss's anger and frustration, the trickle-down affecting Mario.

Mario is a clerical support and works for a large aerospace company that had recently gone through extensive reorganization. Mario is well liked, bright, and has a positive attitude about the future. However, when he talks about problems on the job it's in whispered tones, and a muscle in his cheek twitches. His discomfort is obvious. "My new boss would come back from a corporate meeting and bark orders, 'Do this! Why hasn't this been done? You are the sloppiest jerk I've ever worked with!' You know the kind of abuse. His rage spilled all over everyone.

"I'm a good worker. I've always been given great reviews, and I like the work. Some people think it's boring, but I'm an organized kind of guy. After one of these screaming sessions was over and this boss had stormed into his office and slammed the

door, I'd feel like I was possessed. My head would pound. Sometimes I'd get stabbing pains in my chest. My stomach would flip-
flop. Weeks of this went by. Then something weird happened. I
began stuffing small supplies into my backpack that I carry to
and from work. I began with inexpensive items first—pens, paper
clips, and stuff like that. Then I took more and more valuable
items; my small, petty revenge got bigger."

Not only was Mario hurt, angry, and physically debilitated, he
was compounding the problem by acting in contradiction to his
own values. His actions had begun to make him feel like a liar
and a thief. He felt guilty about the items he had taken, but didn't
feel any better when he had returned some of them. Mario
decided he would have to confront the boss or quit. Neither alternative seemed practical. He sought the help of a counselor. The
counseling process was not a long one. Together he and the
counselor developed a strategy for a constructive confrontation.
But first Mario needed to learn the six conditions for dealing with
anger.

Six Checkpoints

First, one disclaimer. Not all situations involving anger can be
dealt with through communication. Obviously, when anger
involves violence and rage, other alternatives must be used. However, for most situations in daily living, constructive confrontation
can be very effective, *if* these six conditions can be met:

1. Expressions of anger must be directed at the target of the
   anger.
2. The expression of anger must restore your sense of control and sense of justice.
3. The expression of anger must inflict appropriate punishment on the other person.
4. The expression of anger must change the behavior of the
   target or give you new insights.
5. You and your target must speak the same language.
6. There must be no retaliation from the target.

Let's review the parameters of each of these conditions.

1. *Expressions of anger must be directed at the target of the anger.* Mario was expressing his anger at the company, his coworkers, and himself—not at the boss. In counseling he agreed that he needed to confront the supervisor directly but did not know how. So he hadn't considered that alternative.

2. *The expression of anger must restore your sense of control and sense of justice.* Mario momentarily satisfied his anger in stealing, but in the long run it added to his feeling of powerlessness. He was creating more injustice and compounding his feeling of losing control by acting in a way that he found reprehensible. His next step was to be directed outside himself.

3. *The expression of anger must inflict appropriate punishment on the other person.* Mario balked at this one. "I don't want to hurt him," he said, "I just want him to stop." The counselor helped Mario see that a sense of "getting even" was necessary in order to feel better about oneself. This did not necessarily involve any *real* action and certainly no intended hurt toward another. In any situation of hurt, we often desire to hurt others only to ensure that they will know how we feel. "I just wanted him to know what it felt like," was an expression Mario had previously used referring to the humiliation of being screamed at and called names.

The counselor asked Mario if he thought the other man knew what he looked like when he was screaming and yelling. "I doubt it," was the reply. Often simply drawing attention to the behavior may be punishment enough for the other person. Sometimes just being forced to listen is a "punishment." Maybe you can remember the childhood feelings of being talked to. Even feel your stomach contract when your significant other says, "I want to talk to you!"

4. *The expression of anger must change the behavior of the target or give you new insights.* In this situation, Mario had nothing to lose. Worst case was that Mario could be yelled at. He still had the alternative of resigning. If the boss refused to listen or was unwilling to change, Mario would then have the added information that reason and communication would not work with his

boss. He could take pride in knowing that he had tried everything.

5. *You and your target must speak the same language.* In developing his "script," Mario was encouraged to use actual words that the boss had used. Also, Mario's boss was generally a rational person and a good communicator. Again, these conditions do not apply when situations have become abusive.

6. *There must be no retaliation from the target.* Mario knew that his boss might raise hell. Now he began to fear that he could be fired. The counselor suggested that Mario discuss the planned confrontation with the human resources coordinator. Mario wanted to know what his rights were in this situation. He was advised to begin by getting an agreement from his boss that he would listen without interrupting until Mario had finished. Mario was also assured that he could not be fired. The company guidelines for termination were reviewed for him.

Mario prepared well for his confrontation. He rehearsed with a coworker who had a quick temper and a style much like Mario's boss. In one scenario that they rehearsed, the boss exploded and threatened to fire Mario. They practiced Mario's control and response. In the other scenario the boss was more reasonable.

Then came the real thing. The actual situation was tense. Mario began by asking for the boss's agreement to listen. He received a curt, "Don't I always?" Mario began to stammer but continued by expressing a positive statement about having learned a lot since the two of them had begun to work together. This was certainly a true statement. The boss seemed flattered and relaxed a little. Mario then began to talk about specific situations. "I notice that when you attend the director's meetings, you often return angry and upset. You then berate me, raising your voice, calling me names, and swearing." Mario went on, being very specific and using the actual words the boss had used.

As the boss listened, Mario reported that he could see the embarrassment and humiliation in his face. Like many bullies, this individual pretended that everyone just forgot the behavior and went on as though nothing had happened. When caught, he was indeed ashamed. He expressed his feelings to Mario, who listened with relief and surprise. This was the "punishment-revenge" that helped Mario to feel some sense of justice. He felt validated and relieved.

Ultimately the boss agreed to change. And he did. While his basic style of quick temper and lashing out could still appear, it was clear to Mario that the boss was much more aware and more under control. Mario was also able to speak out more quickly to short-circuit any diatribes. They began to work together more successfully.

While each of us must practice and learn which strategies will work with our own situations and style, always try a technique before you discard it. Don't say, "Well, that worked okay for Mario, but you don't know what my boss is like. She'd fire me on the spot." Enlist the help of a friend, coworker, or family member. Review the six rules and see if the conditions can be met for planning a constructive confrontation.

But Don't Forget . . .

Ross worked for a small printing plant. He had been happily employed for more than ten years as plant supervisor. When the plant was sold to a larger concern he was pleased to learn that his position rated a substantial raise. He was also excited about some new equipment and advanced technology that was being introduced. Within the first week after the takeover he received a memo stating that no employee would be credited with more than two weeks vacation time. Reasons were given, but Ross just saw red. He had over six weeks accumulated vacation leave, and he and his wife had planned a long road-trip in their new recreational vehicle across Canada. Ross could not get his new employer to give him the time off he felt he deserved. He was furious. As days passed and his anger and resentment preoccupied him, Ross realized he had to get over it, but he wasn't sure how.

This is an example where constructive confrontation, assertive behavior, and other techniques do not apply. Ross was harmed by a faceless entity. There was no one to confront, no action to be taken to restore any sense of justice. He decided instead to use the technique of forgiveness.

Forgiveness is another technique that can be useful. "Forgive? Isn't that a word for church or hot tubs at Esalen? And anyway, 'they,' (he, she, or it) did something to me that was wrong. I didn't do anything!" Think of anger and resentment like the air you breathe into a balloon. No matter how little or how much you blow, the air fills the balloon completely. So it is with anger—a little or a lot, active and loud or quiet and sullen—it fills the person completely. The balloon, like Paul, ultimately bursts. His breaking point led to migraines, sleeplessness, and family disharmony.

BE SELFISH

Forgiveness is selfish. In the popular *How to Forgive Your Ex-Husband*, authors Marcia Hootman and Patt Perkins state that releasing resentment is essential for well-being. They describe the process as both physical and mental. Consider this scenario. A feeling of resentment enters your mind. It becomes a part of your thoughts, living "rent-free" in your head. Each time you are reminded of the resentment, you feel pain—like probing a sore tooth with your tongue or being continually irritated by a small paper-cut on your finger. Resentment now controls you. You must take action to regain control.

Forgiveness is an action step. It involves completing the relationship with the person or situation; releasing your attachment to the form of punishment (the blame, resentment, the betrayal) of the relationship; and *recontexting* the relationship. The context of a situation or dialogue with another person is like the background in a photograph. Have you ever taken a great picture of a child or friend only to find the background—a messy living room, an unmade bed—spoiled the shot. Changing that background is "recontexting."

For example, take the image of your boss making a sarcastic comment about your work and turn the background into any angry board meeting in which *her* boss is shaking a fist. Or picture an angry coworker making excuses for not meeting a deadline and against a background of all the times *you* failed to keep an agreement. While this technique may not elicit sympathy from you, it does help you picture the situation differently.

Changing your point of view, your perspective on what the other person was feeling or thinking, is also recontexting. This process can change expectations and allow communication to be more open and direct.

"Ha!" you may be thinking. "Just more psychobabble." Do these techniques really work?

Yes, they do if you work them! Focus on each technique whether it is constructive confrontation, recontexting, or forgiveness as an act of selfishness. You want things to be better for *you*. Ultimately improving things for yourself is like throwing a small pebble into a pond: the ripples begin small and get larger and larger, affecting the whole surface over time. By using just one of the techniques described in this chapter you are throwing that small stone, with its positive ripples to coworkers, family, friends, but most of all, enhancing your self-worth and your own productivity in the workplace.

Forgiveness is a very practical word. It has an action step. The action step is to stop talking about the problem. As long as we continue to talk about others' mistakes, we haven't forgiven them. As long as we continue to talk and blame bosses and coworkers for their behaviors, real or imagined, there is no forgiveness, and thus no moving on. Failing to forgive, to confront, to constructively correct, has the biggest negative effect on the person who retains the anger and resentment. You have the most to gain by forgiveness. By forgiving the boss and getting on with the job, you are taking action to improve the quality of your own life. It is a process with a beginning, a middle, and an end. It needs to be done correctly in order to work. Forgiveness is especially useful when someone very close to you, perhaps unseen and unknown, has wronged you. In these cases there is little you can do that will have an impact on what was done to you. You cannot confront "them" or make them aware of the hurt you've felt. This is particularly useful when the six conditions of constructive confrontation cannot be met.

How to Forgive

1. Consciously identify what the wrong is and how it made you feel, how it affected you, your family, your future, your emotional well-being. It is important to be specific. Relatively minor wrongs can sometimes be removed at this point. "I was angry when I spilled copy machine toner on the carpet. I forgive myself. I hurt no one, I was inconvenienced by sixty-nine seconds, and I have more toner. I'm over it." It will help to write down exactly what you think was done to you. For example, "My supervisor ruined my life. Everyone was laughing at me," may be what you think happened. Now write down exactly what was done to you. "My supervisor contradicted me in front of the CEO. She made me seem like I wasn't prepared. I felt humiliated and embarrassed." As you write, some perspective may be obtained. Anger and resentment cannot exist without some degree of self-deception.

2. Make a policy decision, an agreement with yourself that you willingly choose to forgive the wrong—the transgression—for *selfish* reasons. You forgive in order to get on with your job and your life. Forgiveness is an act of grace. You are being a gracious person by forgiving. Take credit!

3. Note that forgiveness does not equate with forgetting. You can maintain and probably should remember what had been done to you. You may choose not to trust that person again, or it may take some time before you can drop your guard. Understand that you can remember the act and protect yourself from being hurt in the same way or by the same person in the future.

> *To err is human*
> *To forgive divine*
> *To forget, foolhardy*

4. Now the most difficult part of this process: stop talking about it. This may be the biggest challenge to completing the process. In discussing this with my coauthor, Patt, I listened to her describe interviews with literally hundreds of women in writing the book, *How to Forgive Your Ex-Husband . . . and Get On With Your Life!* Years after the events of divorce, adultery, or whatever wrong was committed to these individuals, Patt observed, "The stories sounded as though they had happened yesterday. The teller became angry, often cried, was dramatic, sad, seemed to suffer the pain and feelings all over again. I wondered how many times these stories had to be told before they could be told objectively, without emotion, without the drama. Or, how many times they had to be told before the teller was bored by her own telling."

If you find that you have not completed any step, especially the last, limit your talking to one or two individuals, maybe a counselor, spiritual advisor, or close friend. Anger is all too often a social occasion. It frequently disappears when it loses its audience. If the second step, forgiveness, cannot be completed, you might need additional help, perhaps professional. In practicing this step, start with small matters. Recognize when an injustice has been done to you, and use the situation for practice. Give up the "oughts." Don't start with longstanding or traumatic grievances. Work up to those.

Self-talk or affirmations may be useful for accomplishing many behavior changes connected to forgiveness. Try these self-talk statements.

- I have done a similar thing. I remember when I _____. Someone excused me.
- I know _____ did the best he or she could at the time. My single explanation is not explanation enough.
- I willingly release the past. It is safe for me to let go.
- I choose to heal this rift. I declare peace and go forward.

- Let's start over. I'll take the first step by _____ (e.g., admitting my part).

ABC'S OF SELF-TALK

All anger begins with a thought—a perception that wrong has been done to us, that we have been hurt, that someone has caused us pain. Anyone can recognize anger when it explodes. In coping with difficult situations, it is critical to recognize the starting point in the process of becoming angry or resentful. Take the next step of becoming the master of your anger, not its victim.

Rhonda, new to her job in software training, describes a disturbing situation she experienced in her office. Because she works for a large national concern and does training all over the nation, she must attend frequent meetings to receive changed orders, new information, and schedules. Like most meetings, these seldom started on time. Rhonda, by contrast, is always early and likes to feel prepared and settled. She became increasingly angry as latecomers straggled in and casual chitchat occupied the group leader.

What started out as a pet peeve became a major resentment. Rhonda tried to busy herself with work to distract herself from her growing obsession, but found she could not concentrate. She then tried to read a book but felt embarrassed and unprofessional. She found the anger and resentment occupying her mind after the meeting had started. Finally, at an important decision-making point, the chairperson asked Rhonda's opinion. She was mortified. She had no idea what was being discussed. *This has got to stop*, she told herself.

Rhonda was able to successfully use a technique called *self-talk*. To stop her obsessive thoughts, she went through a simple three-step procedure that we call the ABC's of self-talk.

A. When her thoughts drifted to lateness, she said to herself, "Stop! Thank you, mind, for sharing!" She then recited a simple prayer. (A song, childhood rhyme, or poem will do. "Mary Had a Little Lamb," "Now I Lay Me Down To Sleep," "Take Me Out to the Ballgame.")

B. Breathing deeply, she changed her posture, sat more erectly, recrossed her legs.

C. Then she congratulated herself. *Good job, Rhonda.* Even if the thought drifted back in, she simply began with "A" again, saying "Stop," and recited more of her "mantra."

The three-step system is:

A. When the thought or reaction begins, say, silently or aloud depending on the circumstances, "STOP!" Then say to yourself, *God grant me the serenity to accept the things I cannot change, the courage to change the things I can, and the wisdom to know the difference,* or, *Thanks, mind, I don't need your help!*

B. Breathe deeply from the diaphragm and change your posture. Relax your shoulders, uncross your legs, unclench your fists, look in a different direction.

C. Congratulate yourself. Even though the thought returns, you have begun. Remember, as my friend Tom Martin is fond of saying, "If you blow on a saxophone every day, you may not learn to be a good player, but you will learn how to blow it." Keep using the technique. You will gain mastery.

I SEE AN ISLAND

A variation on this technique is to use a meditation or imagery instead of the rhyme. When the thought occurs, say silently or aloud, "STOP!" Then begin a visualization that you have previously practiced. Sometimes keeping a picture of a vacation or pleasant time with your family pinned above your workstation, or in your calendar or notebook, will help. Then proceed with steps B and C.

WHEN ALL ELSE FAILS . . .

Often when facilitating stress-management seminars, Patt and I ask the question, "How many of you have ever read an article on stress management?" Almost every hand in the room goes up. The next question is, "How many of you have read two articles on the same subject?" Most hands stay up. "What did you learn from the second article that you hadn't read in the first one?" Laughing, one or two in the group volunteer, "Nothing!" When we discuss why individuals keep reading more articles on stress management and attending this seminar, the answer is we are looking for something new and, the truth emerges, something easier, something that works faster, a quick fix. To quote Harvey MacKay, author of the bestselling *Swim With the Sharks*, "Knowing what to do isn't enough if you haven't developed the self-confidence to do it."

Recently I found an audio-tape program labeled, "The Six-Second Stress Cure." That naturally appealed to me. Wow, relaxing and ending stress in six seconds. Being rushed, and stressed, I put it into my car player while I drove to my next appointment. The author began by saying, "It takes about six months of practice to learn this technique." There are no quick fixes. And there is probably nothing new under the sun. Research continues to validate the efficacy of prayer and spiritual exercise, the role of community service in improving the quality of life, the therapeutic aspects of pet care, being around children, and giving service to the chronically ill. Techniques that you know sound stale and trite but still work in coping with anger.

At this point in your reading it is probably clear that you must commit some time to improving your job situation, and your state of mind. You must devote some energy, take some risks, say a few prayers. In order to get something, it is likely you will have to give. No matter what the problem or conditions of your job, eventually you will have to make a choice. You will have to accept the conditions or make a change. These suggestions, we hope, will inspire you not to quit, not to resign yourself to martyrdom, but to make a change. You have control over the kind of life you have in the workplace.

Don't let anger, cynicism, and a feeling of defeat keep you from moving on to a more positive focus. If you keep working on yourself you can experience less hostility and frustration and enjoy your job. Author Betty Harragan says, "Failure in the sports culture is not treated as a demoralizing agent, but as a revitalizing force. Losing a game is the signal to practice more, to improvise better techniques . . . to go forward with determination to win the next one."

Recognize

1. Make a list of situations, past and present, in which you have become *very* angry.
2. Differentiate these situations from the next list, things that you resent.

Respond

1. Respond to each of the situations, grudges, and peeves you have listed with a technique from this chapter, or one that you've successfully used in the past.

Reinforce

1. To reinforce your commitment to your own emotional well-being, take this test to assess your anger style. Let the results guide you to more action steps.
2. Consider this affirmation. "I create only peace and harmony within myself and my job. I listen to the pleasant and the good. I release the pattern of behavior in me that attracted this experience. I create only good in my life."

Assess Your Anger Style

This inventory offers you an opportunity to make an objective self-study of how anger affects you and how you deal with it in your daily contacts with others. It allows you to identify a style for insight as well as behavioral change.

DIRECTIONS: Please answer each question as quickly as you can according to the way you feel *most of the time*. Put a check in *only one* of the blanks.

	YES	NO
1. Do you admit that you are angry when asked by someone else?	____	____
2. Do you have a tendency to take your anger out on someone other than the person you are angry with?	____	____
3. When you are angry with someone, do you discuss it with that person?	____	____
4. Do you keep things in until you finally explode with anger?	____	____
5. Do you pout or sulk for a long time (a couple of days or so) when someone hurts your feelings?	____	____
6. Do you disagree with others even though you feel they might get angry?	____	____
7. Do you hit others when you get angry?	____	____
8. Does it upset you a great deal when someone disagrees with you?	____	____
9. Do you express your ideas when they differ from those of others?	____	____
10. Do you have a tendency to be very critical of others?	____	____
11. Are you satisfied with the way in which you settle your differences with others?	____	____
12. Is it very difficult for you to say nice things to other people?	____	____
13. Do you have good control of your temper?	____	____

14. Do you become depressed very easily? _____

YES   NO

15. When a problem arises between you and another person, do you discuss it without losing control of your emotions? _____ _____

16. Do you have a tendency to criticize or put down other people? _____ _____

17. When someone has hurt your feelings do you discuss the matter with that person? _____ _____

18. Do you have frequent arguments with others? _____ _____

19. Do you often *feel* like hitting someone else? _____ _____

20. Do you, at times, feel some anger toward someone you love? _____ _____

21. Do you have a strong urge to do something harmful? _____ _____

22. Do you keep your cool (control) when you are angry with someone? _____ _____

23. Do you tend to feel very badly or very guilty after getting angry at someone? _____ _____

24. When you become angry, do you pull away or withdraw from people? _____ _____

25. When someone is angry with you, do you automatically or quickly strike back with your own feelings of anger? _____ _____

26. Are you aware of when you are angry? _____ _____

27. Provided the timing is appropriate, do you express your angry feelings without exploding? _____ _____

28. Do you tend to make cutting remarks to others? _____ _____

29. Do you control yourself when things do not go your way? _____ _____

30. Do you feel that anger is a normal emotion? _____ _____

Circle each of your "yes" answers in the boxes below. For example, if you answered "yes" to question 1, circle it. If you answered "no" do not record a circle.

Yes Responses

Saint Communicator Intellectualizer	1, 3, 6, 9, 11, 13, 15, 17, 20, 22, 27	4, 7, 12, 18, 25, 28	Firecracker Bully Shouter
	Healthy Expressive	**Violent Responder**	
Personalizer Whiner Sulker	8, 14, 17, 23, 26, 29, 30	2, 5, 10, 16, 19, 21, 24	Nag Scolder Grouch
	Emotional Responder	**Passive-Aggressive**	

Some answers may be circled in each box. Usually there will be more in one than another. The box that contains the most gives the general direction of your style when angry. If you fall into the "Healthy Expressive" congratulations! This suggests you are able to express anger, communicate your feelings, and generally let others know the anger state you are experiencing. You may have a tendency to intellectualize anger, that is, use words to defuse the emotion (yours and others), and at times present an unsympathetic appearance.

"Emotional Responders" tend to react in terms of how they are feeling at the moment. They are likely to get their feelings hurt when anger is present in a conversation or group. This type of response often personalizes anger and sees hurt where none is intended.

The "Violent Responder" style is aggressive and hurtful. Acting out anger and rage is dangerous and hurts others. If you have a majority of responses in this box, additional help such as professional counseling could be useful.

If your answers fall into the "Passive-Aggressive" category, you may be the type who gets even. While you may appear to submit in the face of anger, you may get even with the person on some later occasion, by being late for a meeting or missing a deadline which might embarrass the object of your anger.

Remember that we are human beings not humanoids. Anger is a normal emotion and serves to protect us. If your style is successful, observe and reflect. If you feel anger, either violent or pent up, it is interfering in accomplishing your goals and creating happiness in relationships; some behavioral changes are in order.

EIGHT

Hazardous to Your Health

"No matter how much pressure you feel at work, if you could find ways to relax for at least five minutes every hour, you'd be more productive."

DR. JOYCE BROTHERS

"Make a sign, framed or on a Post-it note, that says: There must be a better way."

The Renewal Factor

More than business is conducted inside the walls of the work-place. The company is similar to a contained city or neighbor-hood, depending on the size of the facility, and has many of the same concerns: crime, violence, health hazards, harassment, trou-bled people, and employment issues. Business spends millions of dollars on these issues, hopefully to arrive at solutions that will in the end save them billions.

Workers expect to receive protection and assistance from the company in times of work-related trouble. Conversely, the com-pany expects us to do our job, act as well-mannered adults, and abide by the rules. Sounds like a fair agreement? It is. Both sides should be doing their best to keep that agreement. It's not easy. Watch television or read the newspaper, and you know that harass-

115

ment of employees continues, hazardous fumes fill a downtown building, a berserk employee runs amok. Drugs and alcohol have yet to be eliminated from the job site. The good news is that organizations are becoming more aware of and alert to problems and are finding solutions. But nothing takes the place of personal responsibility for our health, safety, and fitness. Each individual, each employee must reach out for alternatives and remedies for job issues that affect their physical and emotional wellness.

The company is your neighborhood. Workers move in and stay for a week, or a lifetime. Workers move out, some with severance pay envelopes in their hands. Others are seeking higher-paying jobs and greener pastures. Often our personal and professional lives are so intertwined, our sense of self-worth so dependent on career, that it's hard to be objective about what we're doing, where we're going, what's happening, and who's in control.

THE LINE IN THE SAND

A scene from the television sitcom, *Grace Under Fire*, shows Grace sitting in the cafeteria. Her foreman walks in and asks, "Hey, Grace, been gettin' any lately?" Grace looks at him, laughs, and gives a smart retort. The audience roared with laughter. Many women and men would have been offended by the remark. It was rude and uncalled for. Was it harassment? Was there real damage done? Obviously Grace (or the script-writers) didn't think so. Harassment, whether it is sexual or emotional, is hurtful and threatening. It affects mental and physical health, work performance, reputation, career moves. However, some incidents, like the byplay between Grace and her boss, are simply annoyances. You can take control and see that it does not continue.

Shannon is a married woman and has been an insurance agent for fifteen years. This is her story. "Mr. Wayland and I occupied adjacent desks in the same office space with no walls or doors separating us. For a number of months, Mr. Wayland and I were the only two employees in the office. He was my supervisor. Eventually, Mr. Wayland was able to hire a secretary and a number of new agents. At no time during the fifteen months I worked with him did he ever touch me in an inappropriate way. On the other hand, I did observe a number of occasions when he caressed his new secretary, Anita, in what appeared to be improper ways. Mr. Wayland would put his arm around her, hug her, or come up behind her while she was working on her computer and rub her shoulders. I did not hear Anita complain or ask him to stop. I don't think she encouraged him, but merely tolerated his behavior.

"Mr. Wayland also spent a good deal of time with the female audit staff discussing personal matters. It invariably surprised me how often he spent time with them and how rarely, if ever, the discussion related to our job. Mr. Wayland commonly told off-color jokes in the presence of his female staff members. I did not complain to anyone because these kinds of jokes generally do not personally offend me, provided they aren't directed at a specific person.

"The fifteen months I worked for Mr. Wayland were clearly the most stressful and unproductive months of my career. My experience at a large and important insurance company had me disheartened and doubting my abilities and self-worth, through a series of events caused by him. For example, Mr. Wayland consistently blamed me, his secretary, Anita, and the other agents for events that had gone wrong when reporting results to our main headquarters. On occasions when Mr. Wayland would run out of people to blame for his mistakes, he would simply distort the truth.

"One day he came to my desk and advised me that he had met my former supervisor, Ms. Meyers, at a district meeting. Evidently Ms. Meyers had introduced herself as my previous boss, and Mr. Wayland responded, 'Ms. Meyers, that's not something to be proud of!' When he told me this anecdote I felt really hurt. When I expressed my irritation with his remark, he said he was 'just kidding.' I had my doubts. Was he really just kidding? I think it was his way of avoiding confrontation over his remarks.

"During the short time I had worked for him, I gained over thirty pounds. I really believe the weight gain was stress-related. And to make matters worse, he made numerous remarks about my weight gain. One time, I recall, I was hurrying to the elevator just as the doors were closing, and I heard Mr. Wayland, who was already on the elevator car, remark to the others that it was a good thing I missed the elevator because there was a weight limit. Other times he would say things to me such as, 'Lady, you're about to pop out of that dress,' suit, blouse, or whatever I happened to be wearing. My weight gain was a particular source of embarrassment to me, and it hurt to have him pointing out the ramifications of my extra pounds. On more occasions that I can list, Mr. Wayland told me if I had not been hired before he came on board, I wouldn't be working there. And his phone conversations to other agents were laced with remarks like, 'Let's talk about sex!' or 'I love you too,' or 'You're so beautiful you made my day!'

"Phone messages are vital to the performance of my work. One day I phoned one of my biggest accounts and I could sense he was irritated. 'Shannon!' he sounded annoyed and surprised. 'Why haven't you returned my phone calls? I've left several messages for you.' I hung up and went directly to the receptionist. Her reply to my inquiry about my messages was, 'Oh, Mr. Wayland asked me to give him all your messages.' That did it. I made an appointment with the company counselor through the employee assistance program. After hearing my litany of grievances he directed me to the person who could and would give me the help I so desperately needed."

Who's At Fault Here?

Shannon had been damaged. This was harassment. But what of Anita, Mr. Wayland's secretary? She went along with his behavior. She appeared to enjoy the hugs, the neck rubs. His off-color stories made her laugh, and his gossiping filled the gap in an otherwise boring day. The remainder of the staff thought Mr. Wayland a "good ol' boy." They had a fun group. What was the harm?

Why not take the rap for Mr. Wayland from time to time when he screwed up? It was no big deal—perhaps just an annoyance.

Mr. Wayland was a liar and unprofessional, at best. He got away with his outrageous behavior because 99 percent of his staff allowed it. They too were unprofessional. Shannon had made a wise move to consult with her company employee assistance program. If only she hadn't waited so long.

DON'T ASK, IT'S PERSONAL

Earl had been concerned about Bonita for some time. He thought to himself, *What is with her lately?* He began to have suspicions that she wasn't telling the truth about her absences from work. She claimed she had the flu twice in the last few weeks. She had been coming back late from lunch, and she looked like hell. Her sales had been dropping drastically. She was late again today.

Earl reflected back to the day he met Bonita. "We were both filling out our employment applications, each of us hoping to be hired as a sales representative for a major car dealership. I began a conversation with her as we waited to be called in for our interviews.

"We discovered we had a great deal in common. We had both attended the same high school. I had been a few years ahead of her class, and we had several mutual friends and acquaintances. We swapped stories in the waiting room and in general had a good time. Bonita is a cute redhead, twenty-three years old, a chatterbox with a great sense of humor. I was sure she would make a dynamite salesperson. Well, we were both hired that day and began training the following week. Bonita excelled. Her endless energy and go-get-'em attitude turned what could have been a tedious training into fun. On the last day of our class, at the end of the day, Bonita couldn't contain herself. 'Let's get out of here and celebrate, let's go and have a drink. I know a place in town where they serve doubles at half-price during happy hour.' I agreed that it was a great idea, and off we went. When we arrived I headed for an empty table. Bonita insisted we sit at the bar. She knew the bartender, Brett, and introduced us. Well, when Bonita had finished her second drink I was still working on my first. 'Wow, you really drink fast!' I told her, but she ignored my comment and ordered her third drink. I drove her home.

"On the way home Bonita told me why she had left her first job. She said women in the office were jealous of her. They gossiped and told lies about her to her sales manager. They went so far as to say she was stealing their clients. She laughed, saying that she fixed them. She took most of the client list with her when she left. During the conversation she also told me she had just broken up with her boyfriend. They had been together two years. 'But, that's okay. People always leave me, I'm used to it.' I figured it was the liquor talking."

A few weeks later, a smiling Bonita rushed into Earl's office. "Hi, Earl! What's up? What were you thinking about? You were a million miles away?"

"Bonita," Earl replied, "You're late. Look at you, your face! Where did you get those bruises?"

Bonita just laughed, "Oh, that . . . it's nothing! I just slipped and banged myself on the table as I was falling."

"Bonita," Earl said. "We have to talk." He took her by the hand and led her to an empty office. "Look," he said, "I like you and I've been concerned with your actions. Something is not right. What's bothering you?"

Bonita looked down at her feet and began a litany of her personal problems. Her boyfriend had come back and left again. Both her mother, who had always pressured her to make something of herself, and her sister were not speaking to her. And her car was in the shop again. "You don't understand," she said. "My life is falling apart."

Earl looked at her. He felt sorry for his friend. Because he lived with his brother, a recovering alcoholic and a member of Alcoholics Anonymous for ten years now, Earl had a pretty good idea of what was happening to Bonita. "Bonita," he said, "You can't hide it any longer. As your friend I have to talk to you. Your actions have made it obvious that you have a problem, a severe one at that. Your job performance has been seriously impacted. I want to help you if you'll let me."

Bonita started to cry, "Sure," she said,"You're just like the rest of them. You hate me too!"

Earl held firm. "No, Bonita, that's not it. Remember the way you insulted Mr. Costa's wife at the awards dinner? How about the time you threw the wine at Martin Fuller just because he teased you about not having a date? Your sales are falling through the floor, nobody gets the flu as much as you do, and always on a Monday."

Bonita continued to cry. "I know I drink too much. I've tried to stop. I want to. I just can't. Earl, please don't tell anyone."

"Bonita, I won't; that's up to you, but you need to know that other employees are already aware. And morale has been affected. Bonita, I have a plan. Together we'll get you some help. I'll go with you to see Mr. Costa and you can tell him what you are going to do."

Mr. Costa, the general manager, invited them into the office. "Something the matter?" he asked after looking at Bonita's face. "Well, sir, Bonita has something she would like to explain to you, and I'm here to give her some support." Through her tears Bonita confessed her problem. Mr. Costa heard her out. "Bonita, first let me tell you that I admire your courage for taking this action. The company will stand behind you, and I will check out your health insurance to see if it will cover some or all of your recovery costs. In any event, your job will be waiting for you and this conversation will remain confidential."

"Mr. Costa," Bonita asked, "are you mad at me?"

He looked directly at her and said, "Bonita, if you came into the office with a broken arm would I be mad at you? It's the same thing. You're my employee, and you need medical attention. The sooner the better."

Bonita made a decision with the help of a coworker and friend. In recovery she will find a support group and new direction for her life. She may wonder in the future why she lived so long in torment, and tormented others along the way.

WARNING SIGNS

Smoking isn't the only thing that can be hazardous to your health. Toxic fumes can ruin more than your day. Laws are passed to protect us against toxic air, and if it happens in your workplace, get out. Don't wait until you throw up or your head feels like it will burst. There is no need to be a martyr.

A few years ago, Naomi worked in an office that was located in a commercial building occupied by several medical labs. Shortly after moving into the building, several employees began complaining about what they thought was foul-smelling air in the office. They said it smelled like formaldehyde. Naomi noticed it too. They turned down the air conditioning in an effort to stop the odor. Some of the workers said it gave them a headache. Naomi was nauseated and complained to her manager. He said he didn't notice the smell and that maybe it was the new carpeting.

Naomi insisted something needed to be done. Weeks passed with daily complaints. In an attempt to placate the workforce, management arranged to have the ventilation system checked out by representatives from the Occupational Safety and Health Administration (OSHA). The OSHA representatives found the system up to standard. But, Naomi refused to give up. She knew if she let herself and her concerns be discounted that anger and resentment would only compound her discomfort. Naomi decided to try the chief financial officer. She reasoned that the "money manager" might see more of the big picture. She was right. Her self-confidence and esteem were significantly boosted.

If you perceive there are unsafe conditions on your job, don't let yourself be just another complainer. Don't wait until you or your coworkers end up in a hospital. Create action steps and assert your rights to a safe and healthy workplace.

THE STALKER

Caroline, a branch manager for a government agency, was responsible for eighteen field employees. She was in charge of reviewing their caseloads and monitoring their progress. It was her duty to oversee all aspects of performance. The group was a mixed bunch. She had the usual disciplinary problems: most about the use of the phones for personal calls, a few who wasted time chatting, and some sloppy casework. Nothing she couldn't handle. The lone exception was Ernest Walker. Something was different about him. She had the strong feeling he disliked her, although he never said it.

Ernest was a well-dressed, good-looking man. He was articulate and came across as intelligent. And he was a loner. Working hours began at 8:00 A.M. Ernest would come in at 8:30. When Caroline confronted him on his tardiness he replied, "I work my eight hours. I don't leave before five-thirty. What's the big deal? Why can't I come in at eight-thirty?" He didn't seem to get it. The office hours were 8:00 to 5:00.

There was more. Several times during the day, Caroline would catch him staring at her. Their offices were opposite each other, Caroline's enclosed in glass, his, an open cubicle facing hers. He gave her the creeps. Performance evaluations were a part of Caroline's job. Ernest had been evaluated periodically, like her other employees. These evaluations were sometimes looked on as an implied threat to fire an employee, instead of as means of finding solutions and areas for improvement. Ernest viewed his as a threat. It was that time again, and Caroline was not looking forward to it. Ernest sat before her as she explained the issues at hand—and his lack of performance. He stood up and began to minimize his own problems and accountability. Then he just blew up at her. "You're out to get me and I'm not going to let you get away with it!" he shouted. At that, he walked out of her office.

Caroline immediately reported the incident in writing to her branch chief. The week passed uneventfully. The following Monday one of the clerks in the building came to her office and said that on Saturday morning Ernest had been in the office, which was odd. He never came in on Saturdays. The clerk said that Ernest sat opposite Caroline's office, pointing his finger like a gun and pulling the imaginary trigger at Caroline's chair. The clerk heard Ernest saying, "Pow! Pow!"

Caroline was scared. She used every method she knew to guard herself against a physical attack, but it never came. That didn't quell her fear. She took a week's vacation to calm her nerves. Ernest was given a fitness-for-duty examination, found fit, and transferred to another division. Caroline chose to use the services of a therapist to help her work through her feelings of fear. She only wished that she could have compelled Ernest to seek help. She worried he would transfer his stalking to another woman.

Violence in the workplace has become the leading cause of workplace death for women. Document and report any fears or suspicions no matter how "silly." Note that Caroline informed her boss in writing, but failed to convey the fear and "strangeness" she felt. As a supervisor, she could have referred Ernest to the company's employee assistance program based on his tardiness, insubordination, and other job performance problems. She also could have proceeded with the first step in a disciplinary process. Furthermore, she could have asked her boss or a representative from human resources to sit in on the performance review. By handling the situation alone, Caroline subjected herself to greater fear, a wasted vacation, and severe emotional distress.

When faced with any hazard, occupational or human, it is wise to look for as many resources and supporters as possible. Don't feel it is a sign of weakness to ask for help. The daily occurrence of new and more bizarre hazards make your responsibilities to yourself even greater.

TIME TO LEAVE?

Vanessa, an attorney, had been thinking about leaving the firm for some time. She felt her talents were unappreciated, and she couldn't envision a future with the law office she had joined eight years ago. Once she had had high hopes that someday she would become a partner with the law firm Mason and Mason. Even though she knew there was a "glass ceiling," Vanessa thought she could crack it to become the first female partner. She worked smart and hard, winning more than her share of tough cases. But finally enough was enough.

Milt Carpenter, a fine man and lawyer, had been awarded "her" partnership. She agreed that he was good. However, her overall performance was better. Sure, Vanessa knew that Milt played handball with the younger Mr. Mason, and their wives often lunched together. Once when attending a charitable event, she had seen the four of them sharing the same table. The message was clear. The "old boys club" was at it again.

It galled her that she had told the Masons of her desire to become a partner. They were kind, condescending, and said they would give careful attention to her request. "What do I have to accomplish to become a partner?" she asked. She wanted specifics. When she pressed her request to Mr. Mason, she was told that he had more important issues at hand. "We'll take it up later." Suddenly Carpenter was a full partner. She was angry. Being passed over was a blow to her ego.

"After the years I've given to this company to be pushed aside by this handball-playing jerk, Carpenter." Now he was a jerk. Vanessa began to laugh, "I sound like a jealous wife after her husband has abandoned her for another woman!" Vanessa knew she was a talented lawyer and other firms would be happy to have her. She acknowledged to herself that assertiveness was not her strong suit personally. But in court she was persuasive and aggressive. Recalling her conversations over the partnership, she had been wishy-washy, waiting like a good girl for her superior to notice her achievements. *No,* she decided, *I won't resign. I'm going after the next partnership. As a matter of fact, I'll go to Mr. Mason now. We'll negotiate.*

Thinking things out, taking responsibility for your part, and seeing the humorous side can have excellent results in your coping with hazards of any form. You may not be able to choose your boss, but you have the right to make a lot of other choices. Know that hazards exist in the workplace, just like they do in the community. When and if you encounter people or situations that might harm you, remember that there are people who can help.

Use them. When seeking help for a situation that you consider makes the workplace hazardous for you, prepare and rehearse. Then do the following:

- When you plan to talk, suggest an early, before-working-hours meeting, for fewer interruptions. Also make a clear statement of the meeting's importance.
- Begin with a positive statement, brief and sincere. "I appreciate how much responsibility you've given me." Or "Since I've been working with you, I've learned a lot about. . . ." Or "Thank you for the opportunity." And "You always give me good advice," are just a few of the many positive beginnings.
- Don't whine, complain, blame, or bring in others. "My husband doesn't like . . . my therapist says . . . my children need. . . " are all "no-no's." Stand on your own two feet.
- In line with avoiding negativity don't blame the person you are talking to for the problem. Do not criticize the boss; praise, praise.
- Remember to show the benefits for remedying the situation. You're selling a product or service.
- Be clear. Define the issues that are really important to you. Beforehand examine your own motives. Do you truly want to improve working conditions? Facts and support will be available when you have diagnosed a real problem.
- After the meeting send your boss a thank-you note. Don't wait for his or her action. You are expressing thanks for time and listening.
- What if nothing changes? Disappointment doesn't mean failure. The success is in the constructive confrontation, taking the risk. The meeting was not the end product, only one step. Keep moving.
- No employee is required to take abuse or be subjected to health hazards. Do not be bullied, discounted, or intimidated. At the same time stand up for yourself. Don't blame or invalidate others.

"Much of what we experience in the workplace is not fair; we shouldn't have to work in an environment that violates our integrity and self-esteem. But life itself is not always fair. The key is learning how to get our needs met in an unfair system."

DIANE TRACY

All too frequently job satisfaction is linked to our unrealistic expectations about what the job can provide. We invest our entire selves, our time, energy, health, and family happiness. What can we expect to receive in return that will reward us for such a sacrifice? We must have more realistic expectations, balance our contribution and effort with requirements, and don't expect from others what can only come from within ourselves.

Recognize

1. Make a list of hazards that affect you on the job. Include human ones.
2. Keep a diary of events in the office that may be suspect. Discard annoyances.
3. Recognize your feelings. Have you been concerned, harboring resentments, or feeling anxious and afraid?

Respond

1. What is one thing that I can do to correct a bad situation? (e.g., Simply writing in a journal is an action step.)
2. What am I waiting for? (*The right time?*) How long am I willing to wait?
3. Are there risks in taking a next step?
4. Evaluate your concerns, consider another opinion, then take them to someone who can do something about them. Remember to follow up.

Reinforce

1. Choose the affirmation that fits your situation:
   - My opinions and questions are valid. I have the right to a response.
   - I can say no!
   - I can drop this matter, forgive those involved, and deflect the situation. I practice patience and tolerance.
   - I am as important as anyone else in this company. I am a valuable employee.
   - I will teach others how to treat me. I deserve courtesy. I deserve respect.
   - I have the power to direct my life, my career, and my health.
2. Determine the next steps in addressing hazards. Decide that the situation is important to you. Know that you and other persons you wish to defend have been genuinely mistreated or exposed. Commit to assertive action.
3. Know that you can repeat or escalate your actions. You can state the consequences of continuing hazardous conditions. Make notes about how you would proceed with assertiveness.

NINE

Ring Around the Ethics—
and Other Dirty Laundry

"How would you like a job where, if you made a mistake, a big red light goes on and 18,000 people boo?"

JACQUES PLANTE
Former hockey goalie

"The happy, expansive life is not a life free of adversity nor a life spent in contented leisure. Rather, it is the life of accomplishment, learning and growth."

FREDERICK G. HARMON

Often employee stress stems from unethical and moral or political dynamics in the workplace. Whether personal abuse such as name-calling or harassment, a moral affront such as an affair between boss and coworker, or an unethical business practice such as lying about delivery dates, an employee faced with contradictions to a personal value system is in conflict and thus stressed. How can an individual in such a frustrating and seemingly no-win situation evaluate wisely and take appropriate action? How can an employee deal with the inner turmoil created by the actions of others?

Individuals within companies, representatives of companies, and corporations themselves all operate within an ethical, moral, and political framework. Just as individuals, politicians, and communities have different values and cultures, so do corporations. Whether the source of a moral, ethical, or political dilemma is within the corporate structure or just the idiosyncratic behavior of one person, the employee who is offended by the condition surrounding work, or even faced with serious consequences, will be undermined. Taken a step beyond, the offensive situation can have serious, and even legal, consequences if ignored. How can an individual in such a ticklish situation set boundaries, evaluate consequences of action (or inaction) wisely, and balance personal values and beliefs with the realities of the workplace? Practical ways of dealing with ethical and political realities are an important part of surviving with your job, as well as your self-esteem, intact.

THE WOLF IN BOSS'S CLOTHING

Cynthia worked in a biomedical corporation that prided itself on flexibility in meeting employees' needs. Though her salary was low, the childcare benefits were very high, and she could work a flex-time schedule. She and her husband had worked out a complex but efficient schedule for caring for their two-year-old son and nine-month-old daughter. As a data analyst, she worked independently of others and came in two nights per week from 9:00 to 11:00 P.M. Usually she was alone in the office with an occasional visit from one of the security guards who knew her well.

Getting ready to leave one night, she was quietly gathering up her things when she heard the security locks in the outer office being turned. She heard laughter and giggling. Startled, she stood quietly listening. To her shock she realized the vice president of marketing was speaking to a woman clearly not his wife. The couple went down the hall into his private office and closed the door. She could still hear laughter and glasses clinking. To her further shock she realized the female voice belonged to Reba, a researcher from the lab. Mortified at overhearing this rendezvous, Cynthia quickly and quietly left the building. She alternately wished for and feared meeting a security guard.

As she drove home Cynthia was angry, shocked, and overwhelmed. She was personally offended that a married man, and a boss, would be so blatant in carrying on an affair. She felt anger and sympathy for Reba, who would no doubt be the one to suffer if this indiscretion was found out. Then she began to think about herself. Should she report this? What would she say? Could she just ignore what was going on? What if this continued? Could she safely work after hours without running into them? Question after question began to scroll through her brain.

Cynthia was faced with a serious problem. Not only were her personal values offended by the situation in the workplace, she felt some responsibility to protect the company. A scandal could seriously impact the company's prestige as it was currently venturing a public stock offering. The ramifications went beyond her own comfort level into job security. Was there a "right" thing to do?

If she told anyone, who would it be? Her own boss, a stereotype of the absentminded professor, would probably not even know who or what she was talking about. They'd both be embarrassed. Should she go to the human resource director? The incident would probably come under the category of sexual harassment, and then she'd be involved and have to file a claim. Everyone would know. And Cynthia would probably be the one to incur the wrath of not only the couple but also of others who sympathized with them or simply didn't like snitches. Now Cynthia began to feel like the employee who had done something wrong.

DUTIES AND DILEMMAS

Humberto was studying to get his real estate license. He had obtained a job as a receptionist in a large and very busy real-estate office. Each day prospective renters, buyers, and sellers would call for information on listings that legally required the answers to come from a licensed agent. Often the callers became angry with Humberto because he would not give them information they considered very simple to obtain. Callers did not understand the law and thought Humberto had the information easily at hand.

After only a few weeks, Humberto's manager, John, called him in for a review. John's praise for Humberto's few weeks on the job was effusive. Humberto was feeling great as he listened to the compliments. Then the dialogue took a detour. "You know, it might be easier if you just give out the updated listing information. You could make life easier for all of us. I know you'll pass your exam when you take it next month, and we just don't have the time to be asking agents to call these people back." John closed the meeting emphasizing teamwork and implied Humberto would quickly move up in the company by working in an expedient manner.

Returning to his desk, Humberto sat quietly, mindlessly turning a pencil in his hand. The impact of what John was asking of him gradually filled him with anxiety. Yet John had made the request sound so simple and logical. Clearly *he* didn't feel any anxiety around his request of Humberto.

Both Cynthia and Humberto faced situations characterized by moral, political, and ethical complexities. While Cynthia's situation did not include behavior condoned by the corporation, as did Humberto's, both situations posed potentially serious consequences no matter what action the employee took.

DEGREE OF DISSONANCE

The first step in dealing with a moral and ethical dilemma is to be clear about your own value system and to examine your own motivation. Cynthia began to think along these lines. She was surprised to find her thoughts straying to the executive's wife. She realized that her strong opinions about infidelity had never surfaced before. She wondered if she was projecting how she might feel if her husband, Scott, was unfaithful. Cynthia began to picture the vice president standing in front of a large executive desk with his head hanging low, being lectured by the president of the company, then rushing home with roses to surprise his loving wife. She realized the scene would more realistically resemble the "old boys' club" or a locker room with herself as the butt of the jokes as the executive asked the vice president to be more discreet and take his affair to a motel where it belonged.

Humberto was thinking too. As he evaluated his situation he found himself worrying more about being caught than about the legality of what he was being asked to do. He was surprised at his own willingness to evaluate the risks rather than to simply refuse to jeopardize his career and immediately quit the job. He was disappointed in himself as he equivocated in his thinking.

Both Humberto and Cynthia are evaluating the degrees of dissonance they are experiencing. Each situation contained choices that produced a range of feelings: anger, irritation, anxiety, and fear. The situations also produced the potential for serious consequences ranging from legal ones in the real estate office to simple embarrassment for Cynthia. Both knew that to some extent reporting, in Cynthia's case, and refusing, in Humberto's, would reduce the discomfort, the level of dissonance, and stress. But action would create a new level of discomfort in other areas. Certainly it seemed Humberto would be fired, and Cynthia would have to consider the worst-case scenario of upsetting her delicately balanced childcare schedule.

In the workplace, dilemmas of this nature can simply be irritating. Others can be dangerous and illegal. Cynthia finally made a decision. She decided to consult with the personnel manager. She was risking that her confidence might be abused and the story become office gossip, but she knew that she had to take the risk in order to reduce the level of discomfort she was feeling. The stress had now become severe and her preoccupation with the situation debilitating. She seemed to develop a headache every time she thought about the situation.

Humberto felt similar distress and decided to try talking with John to express his feelings of discomfort. He also presented a way of grouping phone calls so that one agent could handle all the renters and another deal with the buyers and sellers. Humberto was prepared to be fired or resign if John pressed him to violate the real estate regulations.

In both situations, Humberto and Cynthia had become very stressed and found that an action step, regardless of the consequences, was necessary to restore their peace in going about the daily tasks of living and working. Luckily, both received a positive response. John accepted Humberto's ideas and said no more about the situation. Humberto planned to give the real estate company at least six months of hard work and then look for another job. He felt that the company's ethics would come into conflict with his own value system in the future.

Cynthia was assured that her confidence would be respected and was told that the situation had already come to the attention of the president of the company and was being addressed. When, nine months later, Cynthia learned of the vice president's promotion and transfer, she was disappointed but realized that business demands had probably dictated a compromise. She could live with the corporate decision. She and Humberto had dealt successfully with their own internal conflicts.

RUNNING FOR OFFICE

In addition to the moral and ethical concerns that affected the employees in these two stories, political considerations were also very real. Cynthia realized all too well that the vice president had more clout than she did. As an executive he was very valuable to the company, and she might be harming her future prospects by making an enemy of him, as well as Reba, or by being labeled a "snitch."

Humberto also realized the political implications. He knew that he probably had no future in the company. While John had accepted his decision, Humberto saw that he did not personally fit John's picture of an aggressive entrepreneur and real estate agent. He felt he was a political outcast and was ready to accept this and move on.

How many times have you heard, "I hate politics. I know politics are important, but I'm just no good at playing those games.

I just don't know how to play politics." It may be that you don't like being involved in organizational politics. Who does? But you, like most employees, will find it's an unavoidable part of your workplace life. No, you're not trying to become a vice president or run for office. Politics in a more general way is defined as understanding how to influence others to get what you want at work. You may want respect, an expression of gratitude, to be heard, or to find a venue for problem resolution. By learning to conduct yourself in ways that are more politically successful you can greatly increase your ability to influence job conditions. As you gain political skill you increase your sense of personal control, another building block of empowerment. You also increase your preparedness for difficult situations that are bound to arise.

Selling Your Ideas

As you begin to take action steps to assert yourself, change job conditions, or influence the behavior of those around you, it pays to follow the rules of successful salespeople. You are trying to sell yourself and your ideas. An important part of any sale is creating a belief in the other person that your idea will help him or her achieve their goals. "Marketing is . . . creating conditions by which the buyer convinces herself." Begin with the idea that you are here to provide ideas that complement the department's or company's objectives. Do your homework, be specific, and cite examples. Again, emphasize benefit. *I know that if we can resolve this, there will be some positive results in productivity.* In Humberto's story he balanced his refusal with a positive suggestion.

Rehearse your pitch with another person. If the situation has happened with other employees, and they have successfully resolved it, cite them as endorsements. Be specific about the role you would like the boss to play. "When you speak with me, I'd like you to lower your voice, and not call me names." "When you overload me with conflicting demands I become confused. Can you help by giving me only one direction at a time?"

But what if you've tried working with your boss and have reached a dead end. You can honestly say that you've done everything you can. Perhaps substance abuse, anger, or personality conflicts have pushed the situation beyond that which assertive communication can address. The next step may be upward—a political move.

LETHAL LEAPFROG

Going over your boss's head can be a dangerous tactic. It is important to assess what is at stake. Is the issue worth the risk? Assess the degree of discomfort you are feeling. Your judgments and values have brought you into conflict with a person or a policy. Now, how serious is the dilemma? First, evaluate the actual damage to you personally. Are you irritated, embarrassed, or inconvenienced? These conditions certainly can be stressful but may not be worth risking your political standing or your future.

Take the damage estimate a step further. Does this really affect you directly? Notice in Cynthia's situation she was not directly affected. Another individual might have been able to ignore the situation. Discuss your "damage vs. risk" ratio with others. Be open to the possibility that you have over or underestimated the damage or the risks. In the following story you may be surprised at an employee's response to measurable "damage."

Teacher's Pet

Vic and Maila worked for Progressive Savings and Loan before its collapse and eventual takeover by the Resolution Trust Corporation. From her first day of employment Maila could see that their boss, Heather, gave preferred treatment to Vic. Since Vic and Maila were loan officers, they were assigned company vehicles that they were able to use for commuting as well as business. When a new car became available, Vic got first choice. Heather seemed to funnel walk-in customers to Vic. Since both Vic and Maila were paid commission based on the number of commercial loans they brought into the bank, the favoritism seemed obvious and unfair.

Rumors circulated that Heather and Vic had been seen kissing after an office holiday party a couple of years back. In fact, it seemed that most men working for Heather were treated better than the women. Maila could readily see that Heather's biases were creating a problem. Now the problem had become Maila's. She was increasingly angry and resentful. She had begun complaining to all her friends. She knew it was time to address the problem but was unsure of a next step. If she confronted Heather with her observations, Heather would not accept the truth. If she went over Heather's head, the consequences were unpredictable. If she tried and failed, her own reputation would be affected.

Maila knew that she would always get second choice in cars and customers and make less money than Vic. This was frustrating, but not life-threatening. Maila knew she could look for another job, but she liked her coworkers and the benefits were good. Further, Maila did not like change. So, she decided to keep her concerns to herself. She began to address the resentment she felt by reframing. Gradually she was able to change her attitude from negative resentment to positive acceptance. Her self-talk included statements like, *I'm learning a lot about being a manager*, and, *I see my own biases by watching others.*

To her pleasant surprise Vic was offered a better job with another Savings and Loan and left the company. Heather and Maila then began to get along better and worked as partners. Maila realized Heather was not biased against women. The situation resolved itself in time.

Did you have a different idea of what Maila's response should have been? Try to measure the potential for achieving a positive result before you take action. This story presents a case history in which accepting a very problematic situation had a positive outcome. Another approach might have worked equally well. Know that not every situation is immediately solvable nor is there only one correct response. The "right" way is measured by the degree of ease and relief from distress you gain from your action.

Later, after the Resolution Trust Corporation took over Progressive Savings and Loan, Maila and Heather both found themselves looking for work. Heather found a job almost immediately and recommended the company hire Maila. Maila certainly profited by maintaining a good working relationship with her boss even when things were not going her way. Now Maila received the dividends earned by her patience.

If you have made an assessment that you must go over the boss's head to get help in resolving a problem, you might be successful. If you don't act, the damage to working relationships could be serious. While most companies have a procedure for going over the supervisor's head, the action threatens the corporate chain of command. Your boss's superiors must—in a confrontation—back your boss. Further, a leapfrog can make you suspect with your peers and also at odds with your own supervisor. The tactic may give you the reputation with upper management as a troublemaker. Remember, assess real damage, the degree of dissonance, and look at possible outcomes and consequences before you choose this strategy.

But what if your boss is an obstacle, a pain in the neck, totally unworkable, and unreasonable? Run through this checklist first.

1. Break your ideas up into small segments. For example, rather than discussing "our communication" or "my job," you can give the boss bite-size pieces for digestion. Speak slowly and in short sentences. Wait for a response before moving on. Provide him or her an outline of your suggestion(s) for later review.
2. Try to ease into an attitude of acceptance rather than fighting. For example, "I really want to do this correctly." And, "I am uncomfortable with being less than candid. I want to assist you and I can (state the acceptable behavior)."

If the outcome of your efforts is still unsuccessful or unacceptable, you can feel good about yourself for trying one more possible avenue for resolution. You've done all you can at that level.

How's Your Reputation With Yourself?

Very often we don't realize that we can be our own worst enemy. Several good indicators are: the way we treat others, how others treat us, what our surroundings look like, and how we care for and treat ourselves. When we feel mistreated by ourselves or others, it is often easier to blame and criticize than to look at our own part in creating a bad situation. Perhaps we create problems or see them where none actually exist. Low self-esteem is frequently associated with negative and critical attitudes. This simple quiz, answered honestly, will serve as a measure of *your* relationship with yourself, and probably with others. Answer yes or no to the following questions:

1. Are you verbally abusive?
2. Are you physically abusive?
3. Do you often find yourself saying, "I'm sorry"?
4. Do you allow anyone to verbally assault you?
5. Does anyone physically abuse you?
6. Do you make excuses for other people's behavior?
7. Do you seek approval of your personal appearance?
8. Are your friends smarter than you?
9. Are your friends better looking than you?
10. Do you seek friends' opinions before changing your hairstyle?
11. Do you keep attracting losers in your personal as well as professional life?
12. Do you feel like a victim?
13. Do you put other people down?
14. Do you frequently gossip?
15. Do you always need a reason for what you do?
16. Do you usually need help in making decisions?
17. Do you feel you have to justify your behavior to others?
18. Can other people's opinions ruin your day?
19. Are you overly generous? Do you frequently give more than you get?

20. Do you make fun of yourself in a deprecating way?
21. Do you brag?
22. Do you need other people's approval?
23. Do you reject assistance?
24. Are you unhappy with your life?
25. Do you feel guilty?
26. Does life frighten you?
27. Does change upset you?
28. Are you fearful of trying something new?
29. Is your car in constant disrepair?
30. Do you avoid checkups with your dentist?
31. Do you put off medical examinations?
32. Is your closet cluttered?

SCORING: Count the number of "yes" answers.

one to five	I feel pretty good about myself!
six to twelve	I could use some uplifting.
thirteen and above	It's time to do some work on my self-esteem.

Now look at the patterns. Your answers correlate with these categories to give a label to the behavior that needs attention.

Anger Management: Items 1, 2, 4, 5, 25, 26
Self-Esteem: Items 8, 9, 10, 22, 29, 30, 32
Self-Confidence: Items 7, 8, 9, 13, 14, 15, 16, 17, 21, 28, 30
Codependence: Items 3, 6, 11, 12, 18, 19, 23, 24, 27

When a behavior change needs to occur, move rapidly to address the problem. Check local adult education or college extension programs for courses and workshops addressing anger management or self-esteem. Consider individual counseling with a professional therapist. Investigate free self-help groups such as Codependents Anonymous.

HELPING HANDS

Addressing poor performance on the part of a boss or supervisor is never easy. Consider whether or not there are others with whom you can work to bring about some negotiation, dialogue, or compromise. Again, the human resources department may serve as a resource. Does your boss have a friend in the corporate structure who might be able to influence the situation on your behalf? Do you have an influential friend in a coworker who might help? If you have no one to turn to, remember this for future reference. Developing partnerships and mentor relationships on the job must be done *before* problems arise.

WRITE IT DOWN

Being specific and documenting are critical in increasing personal power. Regardless of the nature of your dilemma—moral, political, ethical, or a combination of all these—simply documenting the situation and circumstances is an action step. Documentation provides an accurate base for developing a "next step" should the situation continue or arise again. Too often in the workplace the term "document" is applied only to negative situations with an implied threat of some future whistle-blowing. Yet the habit of documenting can be a very positive one.

For example, relate this to performance reviews. Many employees are disappointed, even surprised, at the results of their yearly or biannual performance reviews. For many, the longest week of the year comes with a lead-footed march into the boss's office for a performance review. Even the most competent and self-assured worker can be rattled by the unknown in these situations. It is normal to fear criticism. Yet these reviews are structured by the company to provide feedback, both positive and negative aspects of employee performance.

By preparing for performance reviews you can create a forum for assertive communication. Such preparation includes adequate documentation. Most employees simply make the "death march" and sit listening in dread or with eventual relief. However, these reviews are not just about you. They simply represent your manager's view of your performance, the corporate process, biased rating systems, and company policies, both fair and unfair (e.g., "This company never gives *excellents*. If it did, what would you be striving for?"). Preparation can change this view.

First, envision this review as a time when you have an uninterrupted opportunity to influence your boss. Prepare for this chance by keeping track of regular discussions with your supervisor, taking notes, and maintaining them in a current and timely fashion. Your memos to yourself should note compliments as well as criticisms. Make sure that any criticism is corrected and that you have brought that correction to your boss's attention, having made a note of the date of the discussion.

Keep a list of your achievements, no matter how small. Note in writing when you have exceeded an expectation, worked on a special team, gone beyond your job description, or completed work before deadlines. Quote compliments you have received form others. To make this simple, keep just one file. Drop little notes, even scribbles, into it. Don't wait until you "have time" to document or write yourself a memo. The rule here is *do it now*, no matter what the form.

Taking Charge

Before your scheduled performance meeting get a copy of the review form to be used. Complete this review of yourself. Try and be tough as well as objective. This may help you structure your notes and lists of achievements. Put them in the appropriate section to document your rating or the ideas that you want to "sell" to the boss.

Then, expect the negative. Remember, most evaluations by definition include the negative. Most bosses feel a review is balanced only if it includes negative comments. If you anticipate the negative you may be less surprised and resentful of it. Make sure that at the conclusion of the review you receive behavioral objectives for the next period. Don't let the boss get away with vague comments like, "Improve your attitude," or "You need more word-processing skills." As a rule of thumb, you should be able to draw a picture of anything that is a goal. The old rule of SMART applies here. A goal should be:

SPECIFIC

MEASURABLE

ACHIEVABLE

RELEVANT

TIMELY

"Improve your attitude" may then translate into, "Reduce your negative comments in staff meeting by 80 percent," or, "Make one positive comment in each departmental staff meeting." Even if your boss does not state your performance objectives in behavioral terms, you can do so after the review is completed. Confirm your interpretation in writing. For example, translate "Increase motivation" to "I will initiate five sales calls per day." Don't be reluctant to set goals for the boss. "As we discussed, you will meet with me monthly to discuss progress. I will initiate that meeting."

Take control of your own future—bonuses and salary increases—by ensuring that your next review will be more productive and adequately reflect your accomplishments. There is no reason to believe that economic improvement will reduce the increasing cost-conscious mentality of companies. But let the review process motivate you to keep better track of your own productivity. Even though the review process may be poorly designed and/or executed, take responsibility and reshape it to meet your needs.

As you read this chapter, you may find yourself saying, *Well, these are all good ideas, but I'm still not ready to take action. How can I make a decision?*

To Do or Not to Do

How do people make decisions? What is an effective decision-making process? The answers to these questions are numerous and varied. Often people avoid making decisions by simply allowing a process to take its course. A wife may deny the evidence of her spouse's affair, unconsciously allowing fate to take its course. A boss may deny the evidence of an employee's substance abuse problem, hoping that some "miracle" will change things. Some individuals let others make decisions for them, saying, "Whatever you want." A throw of the dice, a toss of the coin can create a decision, but you are not then a part of the process. You are, however, stuck with the consequences. Informed and effective decision making is not a secret or a gift, it is simply a process. All success rests on systematic work.

1. First, *probe for all the facts you need*. In evaluating a situation it is important to get the perspectives of others. In dealing with a perplexing, abusive, or stressful job situation it is important to know your rights and that your perspective is shared by others. This may mean taking some risks, exposing vulnerability, and examining character defects in yourself. Evidence gathering is still a necessary step.

2. Next, *put yourself into momentum*. Understand that at the conclusion of the process you *will* make a decision. Know that each step of the process is moving you closer to the point of decision. Envision a rolling wheel or snowball. See yourself successfully moving toward your goal.

3. *Think in terms of alternatives*. Let alternatives emerge rather than trying to arrive at the single perfect course of action. As you share your situation with others some will say, "Get another job." But more likely you will hear alternatives to "go or stay." Listen to the subtlety of others' suggestions to you. Reject nothing out-of-hand. Allow several alternatives to stay on your mental list, including those you might label unacceptable—"Sue the jerk!" Don't defend against perceived criticism.

4. *Don't undervalue intuition.* You know what is best for yourself. Often trusting ourselves is difficult. Perhaps you are juggling denial and self-acceptance. But you are a trustworthy person and you can probably believe in yourself. Your inclinations are probably on target. Listen to see if others are validating your intuitive feelings. Using a process serves to double-check intuition.

5. *Make the decision.* This means immediately announcing the decision to others (depending on the circumstances this may be a limited few) and begin your action plan. Don't wait or you will defeat your purpose.

6. *If the decision is wrong, say, "Oops."* Then start over. Admit you were wrong or that the course of action was too difficult or not realistic. Correct your course and move on.

SUCCESS IS A SYSTEM, NOT ROULETTE

In his book, *The Seven Habits of Highly Effective People*, Stephen Covey writes, "Most people have cultivated habits of ineffectiveness—blaming others, thinking selfishly, only seeking to be understood but not seeking to understand others." He goes on to say, "You must have certain positive habits to function effectively, habits that are the foundation of your character." Fortunately for us all, these habits can be learned.

Covey suggests we learn to: *Be proactive.* Choose your responses; act rather than being acted upon; *begin with the end in mind.* This fits in very well with visualizing the outcome, seeing how you want the picture to look when you finish.

Put first things first. For all of us there are too many things to do and too little time. Remember, "No" is a complete sentence. Evaluate priorities.

Think win-win. There is enough of all we need for everyone. We can all prosper. Be mature and self-confident. Know that you can have what you want without diminishing anyone else. *Understand—then be understood.* Listen to learn, but first learn to listen.

Synergize—meaning, don't be defensive. Try to open yourself to new possibilities. Finally, Covey suggests, *sharpen the saw.* You are the saw and must renew yourself by taking care of your mental, spiritual, emotional, and physical needs.

No organization praises or tolerates poor performance. "Ha!" you say, "Just look at my company." There *is* much poor performance in industry that is not confronted. This is reality, not an idealized perfect world. In order for you to be highly satisfied with your life, your job situation must be addressed. There must be constructive confrontation. This means bringing the inequities, the conflicts, the poor performance of others out into the open. This also means using techniques, being proactive, taking control, and acting in a way that is consistent with your own value system. Only by operating with integrity, self-esteem, good intention, and goodwill can you effectively create a change. Once you begin, you are on the path to creating a satisfying success that says, "I manage myself. I cooperate in accomplishing tasks that are given to me by others. I am my own boss, my own manager, my own best friend."

There Is No "I" in Team

When moral, ethical, and political dilemmas arise, you may feel that there are no choices left to you. It is not unusual to find that certain job titles and responsibilities make otherwise easygoing, good people unbearable. They begin to put so much effort into maintaining control that they become oppressive as bosses and managers. This is the supervisor who used to be a buddy and now rules with an iron fist and makes arbitrary decisions. Such an individual lets you know that he or she has a position with power. And you better not forget it. There are also corporate policies, or unspoken rules, in certain organizations that are not acceptable to you. There are times that retreat is the best choice for survival.

The major obstacle to dealing with a boss, an unacceptable attitude, or a corporate culture that you find unethical is that you will probably not be able to change the person's or group's outlook with rational argument. Don't be a crusader tilting at windmills and do not become a doormat and give up. Instead, find ways to adapt and make changes that will improve your own ability to accept this difficult situation. If you have examined your situation exhaustively and find that you cannot adapt, there is a next step, but first refer back to chapters 3 and 4 on dysfunction and personality style in the workplace.

Then identify the individual or corporate personality you're dealing with. Review the suggestions for working with such a type. Try to figure out the dysfunctional dynamics that are in operation. Has the boss had a tough climb up the organizational ladder? Is he or she under undue stress from certain corporate policies and practices? Whatever the cause, this is the way your boss or company is and will probably continue to be, at least in the time you have to deal with your own unease. Face this fact squarely and anticipate his, her, or their reactions based on past history. *That's just what I expected*, can be your reaction, rather than hurt, anger, or surprise that your efforts or proposals weren't received in a more positive manner.

Pick a middle ground. No, you're not submissive, meekly kowtowing to every whim and order. Nor do you need to be the Rebel-Without-a-Clue, constantly questioning and challenging. There are too many ways bosses can win at manipulative games. Maintain your independence and know that you can take a strategic stand to fight for what is important to you. Be aware of where your moral and ethical lines are. Be aware of biases also. Having decided on this more judicious path, you can go along with some distasteful actions and activities, knowing the limits you have set. Or you may have to leave.

Find a balance between staying out of the boss's way and being visible for the success and achievements you make. Try to do everything right the first time. It may be helpful to get the opinion of another on the directions or instructions if they are vague and if it would be unwise to ask the boss for clarification. A network of information sources can be very helpful. And don't fall prey to cutting down your boss when you make these inquiries. Gossip and backbiting, no matter how satisfying at the moment, will generally backfire.

Also, learn, learn, learn. Even the most objectionable and domineering boss may still be able to teach you a great deal. He or she has gotten to that position through creativity, expertise, or simply pure domination. A sincere interest in how this person is effective can help "recontext" your feelings. You can also learn how not to act when you are the boss. Pass on what you have learned. If your boss never praises the good work you do, go immediately to another and praise their work. Praise your spouse for simply getting up in the morning and going to work; praise your children just for being them. You learn by teaching yourself.

Take comfort in the fact that no boss or situation is forever. Eventually you will part. Know that you want to learn as much as possible from any situation in order to recognize a possible repeat in the future.

Use gratitude. Handwritten thank-you notes are not an out-of-date invention of Emily Post. Whenever successfully completing a step or receiving assistance, *always* write a simple thank-you note. Whether you use personalized professional stationery or store-bought cards, you can't overuse this technique. Presenting this suggestion in a seminar, we were interrupted by a bright young man in a power-red tie, crisply laundered shirt, and braces who said, "I can't do that. My handwriting is atrocious!" Someone (who'd obviously read this book) quickly countered by saying, "Ask for help!" Everyone laughed and several volunteers offered to help him out.

Anyone employed by a corporation, large or small, must be realistic about what commitments and rewards are. The famous English jurist Lord Edward Thurlow, in response to a question, once said, "Did you ever expect a corporation to have a conscience when it has no soul to be damned, and no body to be kicked." While it is true that corporations work best when they reward, appreciate, and motivate, people do nevertheless become an overhead item on a balance sheet. Without the ability to control the costs, no corporation can survive. Survival is reality.

In these days of "lean and mean," the corporation is sharper than ever and even less compassionate. Managers and supervisors are by and large as vulnerable as rank-and-file workers. Employees who are limited in their job skills and who have only one specialty are especially vulnerable. Let go of any ideas you have of corporate job security, or what the company "owes" you. Take an unsentimental look around you. Even if your corporation is making money or your department is doing well, there may be other operations that are failing. Take a hard look at your job. Could it be done by someone who can be paid substantially less? Would the operation suffer substantially if your job were eliminated or combined with another? What would happen to you if your boss or your mentor were fired or transferred?

Many conscientious employees, whether managers or line workers, have come to have an unrealistic view of their own importance in the corporate scheme of things. They feel that the hard work and long hours they put into getting the job done will be recognized and rewarded. They feel that each year these continuing efforts make them all the more valuable. But keep Thurlow's view in mind—a corporate entity has no feelings, no conscience, and no body that feels pain. Chief operating officers, consultants, and accountants are not likely to view the individual contributions on a balance sheet.

It may be helpful to visualize where you would be if your job or operation were limited. Look at your job as if you were in a survival school or on an Outward Bound weekend. Then begin to explore your present possibilities. You are in and not out. Find advantages. Now is the time to be political, to form alliances, to create favors (helping others creates a relationship in which they owe you, if only psychologically), or ally with a mentor. Now is the time to increase your value to the corporation by going to school, taking on additional responsibilities, and asking for greater cross-training opportunities. Teach yourself. You are still in a good position. You can give people what they want, while making sure you receive in return. Plan, prepare, and be realistic. Do not delude yourself. Then there is very good reason to believe that your life, though different, will continue to provide the same satisfaction, worth, and productivity as ever.

Recognize

Write down the fifteen most successful experiences of your life (never mind whether they are large or small). Often people say, "A good marriage," "having children," "quitting smoking," or "building an addition to my house."

Respond

In each experience listed above, cite two or three strengths that were critical to this success. For example, "I used willpower to quit smoking and to keep on with the addition to my house." Or, "It took a lot of patience to rear children and go back to school." Now look for the pattern that is formed. Perhaps you have asked for help from others who've been in similar situations. This is the pattern that should be applied to solving the problems you face at work. In our examples, patience and willpower should be helpful again.

Reinforce

To reinforce success, use the pattern of strengths you found above. In one example "asking for help" is a pattern. Use that strength in a current dilemma. Use any of these strengths and patterns alone and you'll progress. Use them together and you'll see the progress not just adding up, but multiplying!

1. Recognize your own responsibility in each situation. Did you meddle, speak out of turn, unfairly judge another, miss a deadline, or blame the computer. Adopt the "If it is to be, it depends on me" philosophy. *Act as if* there is no *they*—only me!
2. In spite of the problems and discomfort you face, aim for a 100 percent effort. Work to the best of your ability, keeping your productivity high in spite of challenge.
3. Identify the next step up for you in the organization. Identify the skills and recommendations you will need that are essential to making the move. Begin today to make the

plan, and tomorrow begin working at it. If you don't see a next promotional step, you'll have to create one.

4. Repeat the following statements at least twice a day:
   - Today is a new opportunity.
   - I can begin again.
   - The past is not an excuse for my behavior.
   - No one is stopping me.
   - I can learn to forget.

TEN

High Tech Blues

"Once a man would spend a week patiently waiting if he missed a stage coach. Now he rages if he misses the first section of a revolving door."

SIMEON STRUNSKY

"We live in an era when rapid change breeds fear, and fear too often congeals us into a rigidity which we mistake for stability."

LYNN WHITE JR.

Downsize. Cutting edge. Core group and *fast track. Partnering* and *matrix.* These are just a few of the terms we overhear in today's corporate world. *Fax, E-mail, on-line,* terms unknown ten years ago are now implanted in our everyday life at the workplace.

Prior to World War II, change in America occurred gradually. Progress was steady, slow, and easily integrated into acceptable mental increments. We had the luxury of doing strategic planning with some degree of certainty.

No longer. We're in an unpredictable world where technology is a whirlwind. Consider just a few projections as we enter the twenty-first century.

- In ten years, at least one fourth of all current "knowledge" and accepted "practice" will be obsolete. The lifespan of new technologies is now down to eighteen months . . . and decreasing.
- Within ten years, twenty times as many people will be working at home.
- Two-career families will multiply; currently one-half of all families have two paychecks; this will become three-quarters.
- If you are under twenty-five, you can expect to change career every decade and job every four years.
- Women now own more than three million businesses and will own more than half of all businesses by the year 2000.
- The forty-hour work week will become a dinosaur. We will work 20 percent more and sleep 20 percent less than we did a decade ago.

Where will it go, our high-tech world of tomorrow? Ten years from now, every computer, every machine, every electronic process we now use will be obsolete, like much of our accepted business practices and procedures.

But what about our living environments? Our cities and towns? Physically nothing has changed. Or has it?

THE COMPANY NEIGHBORHOOD

Look again. America got older. When did this happen? And how? Thanks to World War II, America became the automation capital of the world. Our assembly lines produced automobiles, airplanes, and appliances faster and better than any other country in the world. Automation helped produce and harvest abundant crops with plenty leftover to stockpile. The building industry raised modern skyscrapers, designed and built ranch-style houses with three bedrooms, two baths, a family room, and two-car garage. Areas that had been open fields were now tracks of homes known as suburbs, with an imaginary line separating classes and races.

The computer was now a growing child. Communication and travel became more advanced. American businessmen initiated relationships with businessmen overseas, trading goods and services. Most important was the information they shared. Exchanges of personnel from one country to the other were commonplace. Jet travel was fast and economical. Thousands of foreign exchange students came to learn at our universities, then stayed to work in our high-tech and bio-tech industries. Our citizens were doing the same in other countries of the world.

The computer became the catalyst for the information highway that would connect America to any part of the world in seconds. A new global neighborhood was created. And in corporations, cultural diversity—mixtures of cultures, religions, races, and social groups—worked together to create a new corporate look. But as we have changed, we have stayed much the same. There is still the company neighborhood. It is a place where people work and mix socially, with unspoken rules, unseen boundaries, and social cliques. As our living environments have changed, so has the company neighborhood.

We're Only Human

In the research department of a respected international biotechnology company, you find racially mixed teams—a melting pot. The neighborhood is not without problems; the imaginary line is back.

The cafeteria was crowded when Azar walked in. She filled her lunch tray and looked for a place to sit. *Oh, no,* she thought, *I don't want to sit with them.* Azar had been born in the United States, her parents in Iran. She was thirty-one years old and had received her Ph.D. in biochemistry from Stanford University in Palo Alto, California. Three and a half years ago she had come to E.T.X. and was assigned to the research and development division. She loved working in the lab; her colleagues were brilliant and creative. The company had the best, most modern equipment known to science. The new project she had been working on showed promise. If successful it would prevent certain kinds of cancer cells from multiplying. It had already worked on some laboratory animals.

As a scientist, Azar took her work seriously. Outside the office she was friendly and open and had a good sense of humor: she had always been accepted in groups. Not so with the men and women on her team. They only spoke to her when absolutely necessary, and often they ignored her completely. Many of her colleagues spoke several languages fluently. They seemed to make a point to switch to an unfamiliar language when she was nearby. Azar could get along in English, Farsi, and French.

Now, in the cafeteria, looking at the only chair available, she walked over and sat down. "Hi! Hope you don't mind if I join you." A few nods were given. "Aren't you glad it's Friday?" she said in French. No one replied. Some began to address each other in German. Azar guessed it must have been a joke because they all laughed. Azar became furious when she realized that her team leader was laughing too. He was her boss. He should have said something. Or stopped them. *Oh, my God, they are laughing at me,* Azar thought, *I'm the joke. How dare they. It's so unprofessional!* She excused herself from the table, her cheeks red and hot from embarrassment. Then the tears began to well up. *"I've got to leave. How can I go back to the lab and work with them this afternoon?* But she did.

In the days that followed, Azar would go to the lab, attend team meetings, do her job, and go home. The team did not speak to her at all. Azar complained to her friend Val. "What did I ever do to them? I tried to be nice and they won't give me the time of day. I'm putting in for a transfer to another lab." Val tried, in vain, to talk her friend out of it. Azar's mind was made up. The team had formed a clique and she was not part of it. In her heart she knew it was because she was American.

Several days later Azar was setting up a new piece of equipment. It contained some glass petri dishes and assorted beakers.

Her grip was not strong enough and the box fell. Glass showered the floor. Azar received deep cuts on her face and legs as she instinctively bent to catch the falling box. One shard of glass had cut an artery in her neck. Azar wasn't too sure how she arrived at the hospital for emergency surgery, but there she was. Pain coursed through her wounds, even though the doctors assured her she would be fine, with very little scarring. Azar lay in the hospital bed feeling sorry for herself. First her job. Now this. She felt like an outsider, an outcast.

Then suddenly the door to her room burst open and in rushed the team, arms full of flowers and candy. They were laughing, talking in many different languages. "You look pretty good," one teammate said in English. "Yeah, not so bad," said another. They gathered around her bed. They told jokes to cheer her. They said when she was up to it they would all go out to dinner and celebrate her recovery. When the team was leaving, Azar called her team leader back. "What happened? I thought they all hated me." "Of course not," he replied, "They were only getting back at you for insulting them in your lousy French."

Like good neighbors, they rallied in a crisis. Azar almost lost their friendship and the opportunity to work with some wonderful people. She judged them to be bigots without ever directly asking what she had done to offend them. Now the barrier was broken.

WHAT COLOR IS A TEAM?

Working in a multicultural environment is often a challenge. The language and customs are different. Azar, a highly educated woman, adept in a technical field, could compete in any job market, yet she came from a "nice," old-fashioned family and was ill-prepared to meet social challenges and perhaps oversensitive to what she perceived incorrectly as judgment from insensitive peers. Remember, people of one ethnic group are no better or worse then another. What are considered manners in one culture might be rude in another.

We can make an effort to learn more about the customs and culture of our coworkers. Explore their worlds and try new tastes, sounds, and feelings. You can broaden your knowledge about others. Seek out their customs, eat the food, listen to the music, and learn a few words of their language. Perhaps, read the history of their country and religion. Express an interest. It's important to listen to what your colleagues tell you about themselves and their families. Get invited to a social event in a home, a birthday party, wedding, or holiday. With understanding and trust, friendship will be your reward.

It's not just the language we speak. Our business language must change too. We have to learn to speak in "techno-babble": ram, bytes, CD Rom, mouse, hard drive, and motherboard. Keys that jangled on chains are no longer useful and have been replaced by magnetic cards. Now we get to worry that the card will get wet, demagnetized, or remain in the pocket of your raincoat. More and more, faster and faster, the newer automation programs and systems change.

Fear of our jobs becoming obsolete is often paramount in our minds. We have seen it happen on the assembly lines in factories all over this country. In the office, where not long ago it took five or six switchboard operators to facilitate the calls of a busy company, now there are none. The new telecommunications system handles it all. The digital voice directs us to "push the button for the department you wish." In the near future telephone operators and the neighborhood bank teller will have gone the way of bell-bottom trousers and poodle skirts.

Reactions to new technology have been varied. Some workers are known to have celebrated the news of a virus in the computer. Others have cursed or cried, knowing that hours of research and weeks of input have vanished in a microsecond. And the role of boss has changed. No longer a benevolent protector or tyrant who hires and fires, the boss too is more controlled by policies and procedures that technology dictates. How we survive the changes and challenges of the "information age" may depend on our willingness to take *constructive*, not destructive, actions.

THE MONKEY WRENCH

Vernon could feel the bile rising in his throat. He took another antacid and noticed that half the roll was gone. He had opened the new package only a couple of hours ago. Vernon began to feel like a salmon swimming upstream, facing rapids and "ladders." Just as he mastered one crisis, another faced him, just short of the top. Last month Vernon had celebrated his fiftieth birthday. Today he wondered if he could make it to fifty-one. Vernon had been employed with Bolton Inc. for almost eighteen years and had been through many changes as the company grew and expanded. He had never obtained the necessary education or had the desire to enter into management. "I just don't like to give orders," he would say when asked why he didn't move up in the company.

When Vernon was hired at Bolton, all that was required of him was to show up on time, do the job, and be honest and dependable. His employment application had been on one page— name, age, address, social security number, level of education, and one reference (he gave his father-in-law). The personal interview with Mr. Bolton had been brief and ended with a firm handshake. *Good Lord*, Vernon thought. *If I wanted to get hired at Bolton today, I would never make it.* Now the personnel department occupied one whole floor. The applications are eight pages long, not including a resumé, plus a mandatory drug test. Ph.D.'s are standing in line for entry-level positions. Vernon had to admit that the younger people coming on board now had a lot of "smarts," especially with this new communications "mumbo jumbo."

Vernon knew he was having a hard time adapting. In the past he had felt safe and comfortable with his position at Bolton. He was looking forward to his retirement at sixty-five, to playing golf with his cronies, and to spending time with Robin, his wife of more than twenty years. Now things weren't working out the way he had planned. A monkey wrench was thrown into Vernon's dream.

Old Wayne Bolton's twenty-six-year-old daughter, Taylor, had come into the company fresh out of grad school and had been handed the job of chief of operations. Vernon had known her for years, a nice little kid who often played in the mail room or warehouse when her dad would bring her to work with him. Now, as an adult, her style was aloof and brisk. When Taylor spoke to Vernon her language was filled with words and terminology he didn't understand. One thing had been made crystal clear: Vernon would have to get up to speed with his computer skills. He had been through the basic training when the company first shifted to automation a few years back. It was hard to learn, but in his job he didn't need to use it much. Most of his work was verbal.

Now the supervisor told the team that Taylor was introducing an entire new system. Since that announcement, Vernon had not slept well. Robin, his wife, was nagging him about his poor eating habits and sudden outbursts of temper. He had always been a healthy and easygoing kind of guy, and he surprised himself at his recent behavior and physical discomfort. His stomach burned and his heart pounded when he thought about the new program. It featured E-mail. When it was installed he would no longer be able to talk with his supervisor or coworkers. The new rules explained that he was not to leave his workstation. No longer could he phone them or walk to their office: he had to use E-mail. Vernon was in a panic. Thoughts of quitting entered his mind. Where would he go; he couldn't compete at fifty. Giving up his pension and other benefits was out of the question. For a brief time, thoughts of suicide came into his mind.

The root of Vernon's misery lay in the fact that he had never in his adult life written a letter to anyone. Not even Robin. How could he tell anyone that secret. His coworkers respected him and now they would laugh behind his back. Vernon was actually embarrassed. His spelling skills were almost nonexistent. Why couldn't Taylor have remained a cute little girl?

This employee is caught in a *techno-trap*. The need for new knowledge comes faster than the mind can accommodate it. No wonder we resent new technology. Discomfort is the by-product. We feel lost somewhere in the middle of the information highway.

Vernon took the highroad. Mustering all his courage, he went directly to Taylor's office. She listened intently as Vernon swallowed his shattered pride and disclosed his secret. "Oh, is that all you're concerned about? No problem. Our local community college has some courses you can attend in the evening, at very low cost. It's my understanding that they feature a class in business-letter composition. Also there are some very good books on the subject. One book that helped me was *How to Say It* by Rosalie Maggio." Vernon left Taylor's office feeling better than he had in months. He was well armed with a plan and clear direction. Taylor wasn't so bad after all!

Like Vernon, you may be experiencing the jet lag of technological acceleration. The faster the acceleration the greater the strain. The stress and pressure you are feeling probably comes less from corporate policy and new technology than from your increasing awareness of the gap between your present skill level and the new requirements. Ignoring the cause of the stress (in Vernon's case, his own weakness in writing and deficiency in computer skills) will only increase the anxiety.

The gap in learning or training must be reduced or compensated for. But this cannot be done while blaming others, procrastinating, or denying the problem. As denial/stress/blaming messages flood the mind and body, there is no room for one of the most profound and self-affirming messages of all: *If it is to be, it's up to me!*

Technology creates stress in other ways. Machines have taken on supervisory functions and perform more efficiently and heartlessly. Is the machine a better boss, or does it, like its human counterpart, frustrate and enrage you? Television surveillance monitors scan our every activity from the front entrance to the cafeteria. In a few buildings even the rest rooms don't escape the small round eye. What's next? A body beeper?

The top brass explain that the surveillance is for our own good, making us more efficient and safe. But is that true? Or do we run up costs using valuable time attempting to find ways to circumvent the system? Often we feel spied on and mistrusted. Most of us at some point take the intense scrutiny personally and resent the bosses who care nothing about invading our privacy.

We feel monitored every moment, from entering the workplace until the "blessed" quitting time.

ARMANI SUITS AND SPY EYES

The little red dot blinked as the TV camera scanned each work cubical. It didn't miss a square inch of the sales division. Junior and senior brokers had been outraged at this personal invasion of privacy since they first got word the cameras were to be installed. Everyone voiced their disapproval to management. It fell on deaf ears. Memos were sent with no reply. Most brokers agreed it might not be so intolerable if the surveillance was only visual. However, this "eye on the wall" was equipped with audio in each cubicle. Every word they said was transmitted to the legal department on the floor above.

An hour-long meeting had been held to explain the need for such a device to the brokers. The company attorney had said, "This surveillance is for your protection as well as our own. After all, you are trading in high-risk commodities options over the phone. We have the responsibility to ensure compliance with full disclosure is made to our investors." He ended his little speech by telling the brokers not to take it personally. "We are not here to spy on you."

"We're not here to spy on you? The hell they're not!" Marcus couldn't seem to get the statement out of his mind. At twenty-nine years old, he was a veteran trader. He had worked two years on the floor of the Chicago exchange prior to his move to California. He took the position at International Commodity Brokers because it was one of the most prestigious companies on the coast and his commission would put him in the six-figures-a-year bracket. Marcus was smooth, fast, and loved to talk. It was a job made in heaven. One of the "perks" he gave himself was free personal phone calls to his friends and family across the country, some overseas! In the past Marcus didn't care if his managers monitored his calls from time to time. The faint "click" on his line would warn him. He would quickly hang up.

Marcus had a problem. His computer was programmed with Tele-Magic. This meant he pressed the *D* key when a client file was brought up on the screen, and the number would be automatically dialed. The system not only saved the company time and money, it also kept an accurate record of the length and time of the call. Now if he called his friends, he had to dial manually. It had been easy to make his call before the "spy-eye" had been installed. All he did was wait until his manager either went to lunch or was occupied with other duties. Now he would have to find a way to beat the system. Not only was Marcus angry at the company for robbing him of his personal "perk," he was mad at the inventor of Tele-Magic too!

He began to complain to his fellow brokers about their plight during the day, disrupting their concentration. After work, when he stopped to meet friends at the local pub, he spoke of nothing else. His friends were fast becoming bored with his whining. It would not take long before his career was affected too. Had Marcus stepped out of his anger for a few minutes and taken a reality check he might have found a humorous side to his situation. Here he was, a successful, young broker earning six figures a year. He owned lots of "toys," lived in a great apartment, and had six Armani suits hanging in his closet. He also had a personal phone credit card and a cellular phone purchased by the company. The rage he was experiencing was not because he couldn't make free phone calls at his desk anymore. It was because he felt the organization had taken away something that was his.

Vernon and Marcus had more in common with each other than you may think. Both were in the process of becoming casualties of the high-tech business world. What set them apart was the action they took. Each produced different results. Vernon used a constructive, open manner, confronting his own deficiency by revealing the problem openly to his boss. Together they devised a strategy for correction. It seems likely that Vernon will keep his job, and progress.

Marcus was also confronted with his own deficiency. Instead of accepting responsibility for the situation that he created, he began to blame, criticize, and berate the company. As his coworkers became more and more irritated with his negativity, word got back to the boss. Eventually Marcus was fired. Marcus acted out in a destructive pattern that cost him his job.

As the life span of new technology shrinks, the rate of change accelerates exponentially. Even the most "with-it" person can't keep up. And some are afraid to try. Bill is an example of an employee who resisted change. He ended up stranded on the information highway. Bill works for a large federal agency. Every month, the employees used to fill out paper travel vouchers, reporting their reimbursable expenses. Although somewhat tedious, most employees didn't mind the trouble it took to get their travel checks.

Then management introduced an automated travel-voucher system. Each employee was assigned a password to log into a centralized computer system where he or she entered itemized expenses. Travel checks were issued in a few days, instead of weeks. For most workers, the learning curve was short, and they were more than anxious to learn the new system because their checks arrived so much sooner.

For Bill, however, this new system became a major obstacle. He had never used a personal computer before and was comfortable with the old way—but, he wanted his check faster too. And, paper vouchers were no longer acceptable. His manager was tolerant at first, letting Bill impose on the secretary to enter his data into the system. Within three months, though, Bill was the only employee in the group who was not inputting his own travel information. The secretary began to complain about the additional burden. Finally, the manager laid down the law and told Bill he had to learn the new system. Begrudgingly, Bill clumsily entered his first month's travel with the help of the secretary. Although this first voucher took considerably longer to prepare than the old paper document would have, Bill felt both relieved and elated at having finally entered the "computer age."

In today's workplace, employees often experience stress caused by the pressures created as the need for technical skill increases. Whether the challenging situation is a software learning gap, a machine supervisor, or a surveillance camera in the lunch room, the question is the same: How do I cope?

THE BIGGEST RISK IS NOT TO

Begin by refusing to be a victim. Vernon, Marcus, and Bill felt imposed upon. They each sought sympathy and a return to the old way. Perhaps you, too, feel victimized. In order to get out of the victim role, we must first identify the behaviors of powerlessness, sympathy-seeking, and irrational blame.

What's Your Victim Quotient?

Here is a short quiz to increase awareness and help you to look candidly at yourself. Answer the following questions yes or no:

1. Are you frequently worried about what might happen to you and your job?
2. Do you worry a lot about the future in general?
3. Do you often feel sorry for yourself because of your job situation?
4. Do you try to manipulate and control others around you by seeking sympathy, crying, or repeating stories of perceived abuse?
5. Do you dramatize events at work and blow them out of proportion?
6. Do you need lots of approval at work and gratitude for doing your job?
7. Do you resent your boss or the people you work with?
8. Do you find yourself whining and complaining about all the things that are wrong at work?
9. Do you blame your boss or other people at work for your unhappiness with your job?
10. Do you frequently remind yourself and others how much you are sacrificing and how hard you work for the company?

If you answered "yes" to . . .

zero to two questions:	You're in pretty good shape; you are human.
three to five questions:	You are bordering on victimhood.
five to ten questions:	You see yourself as a victim. But it's not a terminal condition!

Stop Being a Victim

To end the powerlessness and blaming characteristics associated with the victim syndrome, first you need to understand that you have certain rights on the job. You need to know what they are and assume responsibility for them by standing up for yourself in a mature way. When we talk about rights on the job, we mean more than just those covered by the labor laws. These are rights you have as an individual. You have the right to work in an environment that gives you a sense of your own personal power. Some of us have worked under poor managers for so long that we don't even know we have rights. Out of fear we let others walk over us. Or we permit others to mistreat us, and then we get back at them in subtle, underhanded ways that are every bit as destructive as the mistreatment we experience.

The problem is that our rights are all too often not even acknowledged, much less honored. Some managers who are of the "we/they" mentality believe that, if people are too happy, they will take advantage of management and will not do the job. Discomfort, they contend, is a sure cure for happiness!

Start with slowing things down. Consider these statements:

1. This change isn't comfortable, but I can accept it.
2. I can have negative feelings (be sad, feel pain, be anxious, feel blue) and still deal with the situation.
3. This is not an emergency. It's okay to slow down. I can take time to think things through. I will acknowledge my feelings and then move on.
4. Just because I don't like something doesn't mean it is bad or that it will hurt me. (Change may just be like lima beans.)

5. It's okay to have angry thoughts. I do not have to act on them.
6. I have the right to make mistakes. I don't have to do it right the first time. Nobody else is perfect, either.
7. I have the right to say how I feel.
8. I can say I don't know, and I have the right to ask for help.
9. Practice the statement, "You may be right." Try, "You could be right." "You are right." You may even progress to the dreaded, "I was wrong."

As you reduce your victim quotient and increase your self-esteem, you will, by definition, become more assertive. Assertive behavior is not anger or acting out. It combines the expression of feeling and honesty with sensitivity and concern for the other person's feelings. The goal of assertiveness is not to change you. Rather, the purpose is to give you yet another *tool* that you can use, and put away when you have finished with it. Assertive behavior is used to resolve conflicts, to bring about a change in another person's behavior, to alter a situation.

ADD BY SUBTRACTION

It is normal, and wise, to anticipate certain negative responses to assertive behavior. The other person might become angry, or get their feelings hurt, or be afraid you don't like them. "What if they try to get even? What if I get fired?" You may fear retribution. Common sense has not been abandoned because you picked up another tool from your tool box. Temper your use of new behaviors until you have gained some mastery. You can tolerate anger, hurt feelings, and other responses. Those create further opportunities for communication and ultimately may increase the rapport and intimacy with the other person. If you are truly afraid of some retribution, then some outside consultant such as a minister or friend may be in order. But the goal is to *adapt*, which reduces legitimate discomfort and can help to allay fears. Accepting change while being assertive can give you both respect and support under difficult circumstances. Remember, you have a right to your feelings, and you have a right to ask for changes in another person's behavior. Assert these rights.

Keisha sat at her desk in the accounting department. It was 6:00 A.M. and still dark when she arrived at work. Now at 8:30 A.M. she was still putting the finishing touches on the monthly statements. Mr. Fletcher wanted them for the morning staff meeting. "Damn!" she said, "I wish he would be more consistent with his directions. Yesterday morning he said he didn't need the report, then just before quitting time, he E-mailed me saying he wanted the spread sheets no later than 10:00 A.M."

The hard part of her task was getting used to the new accounting system programmed only last week. Although Keisha was computer literate, with a solid accounting background, the abrupt changes in systems confused her. What bothered Keisha most were the changes that came without notice or a plan for implementation. Just when she had mastered one program, Mr. Fletcher would introduce something new, with the promise that it would make her job easier and more effective.

Keisha was aware that she had talent and was a competent accountant. However, lately she had started to question her abilities to keep up with the pace. She reflected back to the time she had joined RAMCO Media Productions two years ago. She had been impressed with the company because of its clear vision and purpose for future growth.

Mr. Fletcher, her boss, was a brilliant man in his early forties. He was a true entrepreneur, fond of saying how he put up the money and took the risks. Mr. Fletcher moved fast, talked fast, and made decisions even faster. Employees were given exceptional training, tools, and equipment to maximize their efficiency. RAMCO was state of the art.

Keisha had liked working with energetic people in her office. Working for a high-tech, cutting-edge organization was exciting too. Now, behind schedule most of the time, she can't seem to stay on top of her work load. She feels as if she's on the freeway driving seventy miles per hour, and the cars are still passing her.

The job has begun to affect other parts of her life. What used to be relaxing weekends have now become a "way station" between Friday and Monday. All day Saturday her mind is occupied with tasks still on her desk at the office. By mid-afternoon on Sunday her anxiety erupts, a feeling she describes as a heavy flutter in her chest along with shortness of breath. Her mind races and pains set in. "How will I get through tomorrow? What new program will I have to learn? What about the work I have completed? Will I have to toss it out?" Keisha has begun to dread Sunday nights. Meditation, counting backward from one hundred, or deep breathing would not quiet her mind and allow her to sleep. The alarm clock became her enemy. *Do any of my coworkers feel like this?* she wondered.

Keisha's thoughts returned to the present. The spreadsheets were ready. What a relief. Looking up she saw Mr. Fletcher standing at the entrance to her cubicle. "Good morning, Mr. Fletcher," Keisha said. "I was just about to bring you the spreadsheets."

"Spreadsheets?" he replied. "That won't be necessary. We're not going to use them. I have another idea for the meeting this morning!"

Frustrating? You bet! Can Keisha survive in the atmosphere of a fast-track, high-tech company? Maybe, maybe not. Still, she has some choices available. She can resign and find a less stressful employer. She can arrange an appointment for a conference with Mr. Fletcher and explain how his management style affects her. He may change. Most likely he won't. It's his company. One option would be for Keisha to surrender, to "cease resisting, stop the struggle, and give up the battle." Keisha doesn't like to be pulled offtrack. It's upsetting for her to work inconsistently. She takes pride on completing her tasks and "owns" the project. A fine trait in a worker but not appreciated at RAMCO. Mr. Fletcher is a mover and shaker. It is his company, and you may recall he said, "I put up the money and take the risks." It would serve Keisha well to give up her attachment to her projects and cease resisting the changes, accepting Mr. Fletcher's directions. It is not her company, she is paid to do a good job, not to second-guess the owner.

Stop the Merry-Go-Round

Often we take it personally when our work is rejected or changed. Remember the change is not about you. It is about what is wanted and needed for the company. People like Keisha can be far more comfortable when they do the task to the best of their ability simply for the joy of doing it well. We can all take a lesson from a New York City street artist. He draws beautiful pictures with colored chalk on the city sidewalks. Hours of backbreaking work. When asked why he used colored chalk that would wash away or be smeared by foot traffic he replied, "It doesn't matter. My joy and satisfaction come from drawing." The artist has learned to give up attachment to his work and is happy. He does a great job and moves on. With release the artist sets himself free to create something new and exciting. He doesn't look back.

Surrender and release are powerful tools. They are not new. Throughout history sages have told us of their value as the keys to peace and harmony. Their positive results have been proven time and time again. Knowing when and how to use these tools is important. We should incorporate them into our daily lives as often as needed to regain our balance.

When you feel pressure building inside you, stop for a moment. Ask yourself these important questions: *What exactly am I holding on to? A project? An idea? An expectation?* After identifying the sources for your upset, question yourself again: *Why is this important to me? Why do I feel I must hold on? What value do I receive from holding on? Do I want to be right or get the job done? Have I fallen into a victim mode?* When you have answered the last question you will be in a position to release. Using assertive behavior may help you move on. Let go! The process is simple, but not easy. With practice and patience it won't be difficult.

Armed with these tools, Keisha can work more comfortably with a boss like Mr. Fletcher in a fast-changing organization. She can view the challenge of new programs as a learning experience instead of as barriers to her production. She can think in terms of forward progress and exciting new ways to grow. Keisha will be like the artist, working with enthusiasm and freshness, eager for the next new project.

Like Keisha, those of us who are facing the twenty-first-century workplace have heard the saying, "The only thing that's constant is change." Industry must change and grow to maintain its competitive edge in today's global marketplace. Similarly, we too must adapt if we are to flourish. We cannot be resistant to change if we are going to survive. By availing ourselves of the new technologies as they appear on the horizon, we will not only progress individually, but we may actually make our work easier in the process!

Recognize

1. List the challenges you have now.
2. Write down some of the things that would be helpful to you in learning.
3. Figure out what you need to do to bring yourself up to speed (attend seminars, read books).
4. What feelings do you attach to these challenges?

Respond

1. Buy a journal to record your feelings and reactions in regard to lack of control, powerlessness, and dysfunctional roles.
2. Decide to upgrade your job skills through a class, career counseling, or tutoring.
3. Consider getting more information on stress management—a book, a class, the employee assistance program, or other avenues for personal counseling.
4. Dialogue with yourself:
   - Am I doing my best work?
   - Do I expect my boss or coworkers to change?
   - Do I expect the company to change?

- Do I want more encouragement?
- Do I want more training?

5. Listen more carefully to others. Notice that you may be responding when you don't need to. Wait for questions to be asked.

Reinforce

1. Try making these statements to yourself:
   - I ask questions and express my feelings directly.
   - Today I listen. I have the strength to be still.
   - I can learn new skills. I can be exactly what I want to be.
   - I am valuable. I am more valuable as part of a team.
2. Make ten 3 × 5 cards with phrases your boss uses that make it hard for you to cope with the job. You will then be able to respond when the occasion arises. For example, "When you raise your voice, I feel like a little kid." Or, "There's something I want to say, and I need your agreement that you will listen, not react."

ELEVEN

Seize the Moment: Rekindling the Excitement

"You have brains in your head.
You have feet in your shoes.
You can steer yourself any direction you choose . . . "

DR. SEUSS

"If you don't know where you are going, you will surely
arrive there."

ANN D. CLARK, Ph.D.

As creative human beings, we have the need to search and reach for new challenges in our lives. We are constantly planning: a vacation, a family, a different home. As curious creatures we want to know and learn. We are challenged to learn to speak a new language or drive a car, to relax more or develop more patience. As visionaries we dream of a future free from family worries, financial problems, and self-doubt. In moments of insight, we make promises to ourselves to be more, do more, and have more. But very often these are promises we somehow don't carry out.

Remember all those New Year's resolutions you forgot by Valentine's Day? Or those times when you swore, "I have to change my ways." How about that new skill you were going to perfect, or that diet you've been on since birth? What happened to the idea about opening your own business, or becoming an author? For whatever reason we made these promises to ourselves—out of desperation or with good intention—we often give them up as quickly as we make them. Why do we give up our dreams so easily?

To Err Is . . . Great!

We view mistakes as a sign of failure, forgetting that errors are essential to our learning process. If we possessed all knowledge, there would be no need for schools or teachers. If we were equipped with all skills, practice would be unnecessary. When research scientists make errors, they are called experiments. From each error valuable lessons are learned that further advance the research. The process is examined, and the errors are used to determine the design of the next procedure. Each experiment leads closer to the intended results. Success is not defined by the elimination of all the errors, but rather as progress toward a goal.

Sports provides a similar model. Athletes use losses, training lapses, criticism as motivation to train harder, to try again, to improve technique. They hold on to the goals and dreams. Yet most of us are more often defeated by slips and self-defined failures. Too often we fail to allow ourselves room for mistakes. We abort our project, abandon the goal at the first backslide.

Millions of people begin new diets each day only to give them up by noon. Ms. Dieter happens to slip up and munch a piece of candy at 10:15 A.M. Instead of getting right back on track, she may abandon the whole diet saying, "It's no use, I blew it." If you don't spend every waking moment zealously aiming toward your target, so what? Take the loss in stride and stay the course. When a jet is guided by radar, it flies only a theoretical straight line. In fact, it veers, errs perhaps, constantly correcting to remain on course. Jets may be seen as off course 90 percent of the time, yet always moving in the right direction. Sailboats, too, tack back and forth in the channel to pick up the wind. If *you* begin to drift off course, you may have to make adjustments to get where you're going. Continue to correct your course and keep your attention on the goal you have set.

Having done an evaluation of yourself as an employee, your company, your boss, and your coworkers, now is the time to implement changes into your job, your attitude, and your behavior. From a list of the Three Rs' action steps and changes, you can evolve an action plan. Try to accomplish some small steps each day. Evaluate the ones that don't work, and renegotiate with yourself. Put off some steps for later action.

Prioritize your goals according to importance and immediacy. Select the action steps needed to achieve the goals. Take the smallest steps first to gather momentum. Be ready to receive others' responses. Be open to praise and compliments as well as negative responses. Remember that as you change, others will struggle to keep you from doing so. Reevaluate your goals quarterly and regularly. Share your achievements, however small, with trusted supporters.

ISOLATION TRAPS

Be persistent and stick with the process. People may not want to change or see you change. They may be invested in the way you are. Your poor performance may make them look good. Codependency may be useful to them. If you begin working better, faster, smarter, they may feel threatened. Avoid the critics and wet blankets. Find cheerleaders instead. Letting coworkers know you are working on a self-improvement plan may ease their perceptions of being threatened. Enlist their support in your tasks. Ask for their suggestions and learn from them, both what to do and what not to do. Make coworkers into your change coaches, or makeover models. Motivation is the key to perseverance. Your success begins when you start it. Success has no end. It is a rolling stone that can keep on going as long as you are providing momentum.

"But," you say, "I'm all fired up now, but what about six months from now? How can I keep going." Motivation is the *by-product* of desire. Notice that nobody wants cottage cheese and carrot sticks for lunch: it is the vision of "washboard abs" or pictures of a trimmer you that is desired, and *that* provides motivation! Again, use planning and process to create motivation at those times when work mounts up, tempers flare, or organizational charts start circulating. Avoid the isolating and demotivating traps of bad habits, your own comfort zone, denial, "group think," or the general press of life. See your goals as the bull's-eye on a dartboard. Target your vision.

Melissa had been with the same company for over five years and had held four different positions. When she moved to marketing, the grapevine opinion was that she had finally met a manager who wouldn't put up with her attitude and poor performance. True enough. After thirty days she was written up, after forty-five she was in human resources and referred for counseling, and after sixty days she was put on last-chance probation. Five days into the probation she was fired.

One problem with Melissa was her feeling of invincibility. She felt, after five years of service to the company, that no one would fire her. Her example proved to her coworkers that length of service does not equal job security. During her exit interview, Melissa complained that none of her previous bosses had complained about her performance. In actuality, none of them had done so on the record or directly to her. She was allowed to continue performing dysfunctionally in each position she held, until she was transferred to another department. A common problem with companies is not knowing what to do with a problem employee. But Melissa knew she had a problem. It was her own denial, her lazy habits, her rationalization that made her continue underperforming and ultimately become a "surprised victim." One option suggested by the employee assistance firm working with the company was to have several coworkers doing jobs similar to Melissa's coach her for several hours during the day. She needed to revamp her attitude, her behavior, and her skills. Melissa preferred to stick with her victim posture.

Jane worked for an alcoholic boss. He would be fine for several months and then begin drinking at lunch or in the morning. Jane began to notice and finally spoke of the behavior to coworkers who said his behavior had gone on for years. He was a partner in the company, so nothing would be done. Jane began to resent her boss, to disrespect him, and finally to despise him during these drinking bouts. She threw memos down, slammed doors, "lost" his messages, was rude to him, and considered calling the police to catch him drinking and driving on his way home.

Eventually, one of the other partners took Jane aside and let her know that if her disrespectful behavior continued they would have to let her go. Jane had to do something to come to terms with her emotional turmoil. She had to learn to accept her boss, to respect him again, the way she had when she first started working there. The first step for Jane was to admit that her behavior had to change. Her job was at stake, not his. She could not change her boss, but she could change her attitude, her perceptions, her actions.

Jane learned to act professionally. Her focus on professionalism allowed her to see how her own behavior could change. She asked herself how she would act if the problem was not alcohol but simply a difficult personality. She began to look at her position as a career and a challenge rather than just a job in which she had to "take it." This, rather than her boss's appreciation, became her motivation for quality and excellence.

Jane began to attend Alcoholics Anonymous meetings and learned how to accept her alcoholic boss and get on with her job. She learned to set boundaries and limits, and found out what was acceptable to her. She listened to stories from others who had overcome similar problems. Looking back, Jane feels grateful to her former boss. "If it had not been for his drinking problem, I would not have had the impetus to work on my own issues. The experience was a challenge that taught me a lot about survival."

Regain the joy in the job. Make a list of things in your job that do (or used to) give you joy, satisfaction, happiness, or elation. Focus on these. Create your own affirmations and say them daily with real feeling (fake it if necessary). Affirmations spoken in a hopeless or sarcastic tone are less effective than those issued forth with meaning and force.

"Today I will find joy in my work!"

HITTING THE BULL'S-EYE

Think of targeting as a circular process. You begin by choosing a specific goal or target; develop the action steps, and visualize your targeting as a flexible process. Here's an example. Mary says, "I want to get my real estate license. My plan is to go to real estate school and pass the state exam." Next she takes action by carrying out the first step of her plan. She enrolls in school and completes her first three classes. By the third class Mary feels the

TARGETING YOUR GOAL

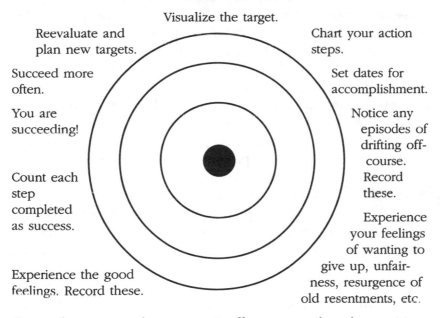

Visualize the target.

Reevaluate and plan new targets.

Chart your action steps.

Succeed more often.

Set dates for accomplishment.

You are succeeding!

Notice any episodes of drifting off-course. Record these.

Count each step completed as success.

Experience your feelings of wanting to give up, unfairness, resurgence of old resentments, etc.

Experience the good feelings. Record these.

Correct the course and move on. Reaffirm your goals and your vision.

material is too difficult for her to learn. She misses the next class because of her son's birthday party, and by the fifth class, she thinks she's too far behind to catch up.

Mary feels like quitting but decides not to give up. She reaffirms her goal and continues with her studies. She doesn't label her difficulty as failure. She visualizes herself closing big deals. She feels better about herself for going through the barrier, and to her surprise, the real estate course begins to make more sense. She completes her studies and passes the exam. Mary confidently plans her new target. "Now I want to work for the most productive real estate company in town."

Perseverance is an admirable quality. However, there is a difference between persevering and being stubborn, holding on to something, or attempting to put square pegs into round holes. If your dream begins to turn into a nightmare, stop. Take a long, hard look at what you're doing. If you have been unrealistic, reevaluate. Is your plan adversely affecting your physical well-being or mental health? Are you experiencing more instead of fewer problems? Do minor irritations upset you more than they used to? Do you cry more often? Is your goal affecting your home life? Are you having frequent arguments with your family? It's time for you to reassess your situation. You may have to give up that goal for now. More likely, you will be able to overcome the problems by altering your method or practicing more flexibility in your plans.

Consider a football game. A specific target is designated. All the players are in agreement as to the goal. The quarterback calls the play. A long, downfield pass may get there quickly, but there are obstacles along the way. On the football field, they are called defensive backs, free safeties, and defensive linemen. When running into (or passing into) these obstacles, the quarterback may elect to throw a short, sideline pass. It may look as if the team is off course. If the game plan works, eventually the target is reached. Whichever team reaches the goal most often within an allotted time is declared the winner. Just as in football, when you are targeting, you may have to alter strategies, go for the short pass, or simply kick a field goal.

Where's the Beef?

Many times we don't take the time to design a plan of action. We haven't worked out the day-by-day steps to achieve the intended result. Lacking a plan, we may also lack sufficient commitment. Without a plan, commitment, and the steps to move toward a goal, we may not understand what's required to attain our results. We give in to frustration and confusion. As we search for an easier, softer way, we become fatigued. We would rather quit than risk what we have visualized as failure. It seems easier to give up. Often we overlook the most important factor in reaching our targets—a clear picture of what we want to accomplish. Remind yourself of the rewards. Literally draw a picture of yourself where you want to be. Put that picture where you see it daily. The bathroom mirror is a good choice. Remind yourself that motivation is the by-product of desire. As you increase the desire for your goal, motivation is also increased.

Fancy Footwork

The benefits you will gain from working your "Basic Plan," the beginning of the targeting process, are numerous. First, the benefits are not primarily seen in changes on the job but in how you feel about yourself. The gains in self-esteem are the most valuable of all. You will find release from anger (especially at yourself), from resentments turned inward, from depression turned outward. You will gain a renewed sense of self-honesty, your own values, standards, and personal morality. You will no longer be working against your own value system.

Self-discipline is yet another gain. As you progress in targeting and accomplishing your action steps, you will feel in greater control of your emotions, less affected by the actions, attitudes, and opinions of others. Instead of leading with your emotional chin, you are now executing a series of planned, controlled moves. In the language of boxing, you're displaying some fancy footwork and you're less likely to be hit.

Through empowerment you will gain increased control—if only in your perception. It is likely you will have gained increased control over your work environment. You will influence and persuade others more effectively and find yourself more productive, not only on the job, but in the personal and social spheres of your life as well. Dreams, not fear and desperation, will move us to a higher level of performance.

CALL ALLIED VAN LINES

Sometimes you have a job or a situation that cannot be remedied. Your efforts to change become a greater struggle. Things continue to happen that seem to be out of your control. Pressure mounts, last-minute crises arise, appointments are missed, papers get misplaced, and projects are covertly sabotaged.

Hedy was the office manager of a small, thriving business. She talked many times about getting married and moving out of the state. Run-ins with her boss were becoming more frequent, and she was having trouble getting along with the rest of the staff. One of Hedy's duties was to coordinate the inner-office communication system. On hearing about the proposed new phone equipment, she protested vehemently, saying that such a change wasn't necessary, that it would be too complicated for the staff, and that the old system was quite adequate, thank you.

But the company installed the system, and a phone company representative came to instruct the staff on its usage. Hedy was noticeably absent for most of the session, home with a cold. When she did attend, she seemed disinterested, hostile, and would not interact with the trainer. Once left on her own, Hedy could not handle the new phone system. Long-distance callers were cut off and had to be recontacted. Phone lines were out of service for hours at a time. Calls were crossed. Confusion reigned. Stress levels rose. Callers became irate, resulting in business losses. Tempers flared within the office.

Hedy was ultimately fired. At some level she knew her unwillingness to open her mind to something new created chaos. Her desire to be somewhere else left her mind scattered. Had she accepted the new vision instead of drawing a line in the corpo-rate sand, the changeover would have been much smoother, and Hedy could have been a hero. Everyone concerned could have been saved the grief, stress, and confusion. But, she could not re-target, or change her own vision.

When things fall apart in relationships, we often beat our-selves up for not paying attention to the warning signs. "Why didn't I see that sooner?" But pain can indeed create gain, and we can use what we have learned, what we need to know, to ensure success in our next venture.

It's Time to Move On

Are you fed up? Angry? Disillusioned? Perhaps your needs have not been met or you can't see any future to your job. Okay, quit. You have that right. Before you slam the door behind you, over-loaded with your belongings, give this decision-making exercise a try.

First take a legal-size piece of paper and draw a line down the middle, from top to bottom. On the right side of the paper write down everything you like about your job, excluding your salary. Now on the left write down everything you perceive as being wrong—those things that do not meet your needs. When you have finished you will have enough information to make a conscientious choice.

If your decision is to leave, make sure you cover yourself by doing your best work in the time you have left. It can pay off with a good recommendation. Do your job search outside the work-place. If you don't you may find yourself leaving sooner than planned. Your coworkers may overhear and inform your super-visor just to score points with her. Besides, it's dishonest. You're still on the payroll. It's not on your time. When you were hired you sold your time—the company bought it. Make phone calls on your lunch hour or break, and be sure you do so outside the building. Send letters of inquiry and resumés to potential employ-ers. Plan ahead when you're ready to resign. Your inappropriate actions now will hurt you down the road. Be professional by writing your letter of resignation. Give careful consideration to your personal career needs before stating your decision. Give at least two weeks' notice. Don't be surprised if you are asked to leave immediately and told you can pick up your personal items after the close of business. Be prepared financially. Don't count on that extra two weeks' pay you thought you would have coming to you. The company will only allow you to continue to work when it is to their advantage.

You don't have to feel guilty about leaving or letting the company down. Take care of yourself first. Someone will take your place. You hopefully made a positive difference while you were employed, and you will carry all your good qualities to your next position. The company is impersonal; coworkers are not. Don't leave them with a mess to clean up. Quit with dignity and integrity for yourself and the possibility of future jobs. When you follow these do's and don'ts you will start your next position clean, fresh, and feeling good about yourself.

But no matter how long you choose to stay with a job, it's important to be objective. In business, as in life, it's easy to become complacent, to go with the flow. But isn't it better to be in control? You bet!

So look at the big picture. At the beginning of each year, put notes on your calendar to do a job evaluation in the months of June and January. You get reviewed by your boss, right? In turn, there's nothing wrong, and everything right, with reviewing your job, your boss, the people you work with, and maybe even yourself. You may be surprised about what you learn. There are no rules here, so be as creative as you like. You're the boss! Ask some tough questions. And answer them truthfully. How do I feel about my job? What am I doing? Is everything okay here? Am I being treated well? Am I financially sound? Can I do better? Do I want more? Is this a healthy environment?

A problem is usually a gift in disguise, if you are willing to recognize it as such. If you've been hanging on to a job you no longer want, you're probably creating many of the challenges you've been having with your boss or your coworkers. If you're tired of the relationship, you may find more and more irritations creeping in. Discomfort in our lives can bring awareness into conscious thought. When it's time to move, start packing.

In the preceding chapters we have described management— boss management, anger management, self-management. If it is time to go, that becomes the action plan. Often making the decision to leave, voicing it to family and friends, creates a sense of relief and renews the energy needed to target a new job—a new vision for you. In making the decision to move on, it is necessary to be rigorously honest with yourself. Tell the truth about what you are and are not willing to do. If the task, whatever it may be, honestly, seems hopeless, let it go. If, like Hedy, you are not willing to change in the workplace, move on rather than resist. Give yourself permission to stay as you are and take a next step. If you are not willing to take the risks you perceive as necessary to gain control, let that be a statement of self-understanding, not self-criticism. Finding your niche then becomes the target.

Promises, Promises . . .

In *The Big Book* of Alcoholics Anonymous, a very powerful section is popularly referred to as, "The Promises." The section begins, "If we are painstaking about this phase of our development, we will be amazed before we are halfway through. We are going to know a new freedom and a new happiness. We will not regret the past nor wish to shut the door on it. We will comprehend the word serenity and we will know peace." As *The Big Book* has promised hope to millions, we promise that to you. You can change your life. You can increase your ability to find control where there seems to be no opportunity for power. You can feel good about yourself, your job, and your coworkers, including the boss. You can survive the problems, the challenges, the obstacles, and get on with your life!

Bibliography

Alcoholics Anonymous, *The Big Book*. Alcoholics Anonymous World Services, 1976.

Bramson, R. *Coping With Difficult People*. Anchor Press, 1981.

Clark, Ann D. *Looking Good*, Hazelden, 1990.

Fensterheim, H. and J. Baer. *Don't Say Yes When You Want to Say No*. Dell Books, 1975.

Fisher, R. and W. Ury. *Getting to Yes: Negotiating Agreement Without Giving In*. Penguin Books, 1983.

Folger, J. and M. Poole. *Working Through Conflict: A Communication Perspective*. Scott, Foresman, 1984.

Follman, J. F. *Helping the Troubled Employee*. Amacom, 1978.

Gawain, S. *Creative Visualization*. Bantam Books, 1978.

Harmon, Frederick G. *The Executive Odyssey: Secrets for a Career Without Limits*. John Wiley and Sons, 1989.

Harragan, Betty Lehan. *Games Mother Never Taught You, Corporate Gamesmanship for Women*. Warner Books, 1977.

Harris, T. A., *I'm OK–You're OK*. Harper & Row Publishers, Inc., 1973.

Hootman, Marcia, and Patt Perkins. *How to Forgive Your Ex-Husband*, Doubleday, 1982.

MacKay, Harvey. *Swim With the Sharks Without Being Eaten Alive*, William Morrow, 1988.

Marston, W. M. *Emotions of Normal People*. Persona Press, 1979.

Peck, M. S. *The Road Less Traveled: A New Psychology of Love, Traditional Values and Spiritual Growth*. Simon & Schuster, 1978.

Seuss, Dr. *Oh, The Places You'll Go!*. Random House, 1990.

Steven Covey, *The Seven Habits of Highly Successful People*, Simon & Schuster, 1989.

Wells, T. *Keeping Your Cool Under Fire: Communicating Non-Defensively*. McGraw-Hill, 1980.

Woitilz, Janet. *Adult Children of Alcoholics*. Health Communications, Inc., 1983.

Index